THE
ART
OF
DOING

THE
ART

OF

DOING

A GUIDE TO GETTING MOTIVATED, GETTING UNSTUCK AND GETTING IT DONE

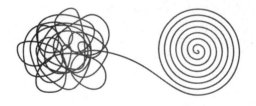

JESSE
LIPSCOMBE

Collins

Published by Collins, an imprint of HarperCollins Publishers Ltd

First edition

HarperCollins books may be purchased for educational, business,
or sales promotional use through our Special Markets Department.

HarperCollins Publishers Ltd
Bay Adelaide Centre, East Tower
22 Adelaide Street West, 41st Floor
Toronto, Ontario, Canada
M5H 4E3

www.harpercollins.ca

Library and Archives Canada Cataloguing in Publication

Title: The art of doing : a guide to getting motivated, getting unstuck and getting it done
/ Jesse Lipscombe.
Names: Lipscombe, Jesse, author.
Description: First edition. | Includes bibliographical references.
Identifiers: Canadiana (print) 20240464117 | Canadiana (ebook) 20240469410 |
ISBN 9781443470889 (softcover) | ISBN 9781443470896 (Ebook)
Subjects: LCSH: Motivation (Psychology) | LCSH: Self-actualization (Psychology) |
LCSH: Self-realization. | LCGFT: Self-help publications.
Classification: LCC BF637.S4 L57 2025 | DDC 158.1—dc23

Printed and bound in the United States of America
24 25 26 27 28 LBC 5 4 3 2 1

For anyone who has ever dreamed of doing more,
who believes that they were meant for bigger things,
who has lost the fire, the drive and the hunger,
who feels like time is running out.
This book is for you.
It's for you, for me and for anyone who needs a little push
to get to where they've always wanted to go.

CONTENTS

THE

ART

OF

DOING

INTRODUCTION

The *Art of Doing* is as much a lifestyle, practice and philosophy as it is a story. My story: the story of a regular guy who dared to do remarkable things.

This book takes lessons from my elementary-aged self, the kid who started a blackjack casino during recess so he could win better snacks. It follows the ups and downs of my life as a young actor in Alberta who, at fourteen, starred alongside legendary actor Sidney Poitier and years later, at thirty-eight, sweat buckets with Kevin Hart. It follows my entrepreneurial journey as I founded over fifteen companies, the earliest at age sixteen. This book captures nuggets of wisdom from my life as a professional athlete on the world's stage, at one time ranking in the top ten. It also presents the tools I used to graduate from a C-level English student to a published author.

Together, we will tear down some of your creative barricades, just like I tore through mine. You'll see how I was able to make courageous strokes into the visual art world, turning my passions into commissioned works and lucrative endeavours. I'll explain what it took to create an international, anti-discriminatory movement that helped prepare a country years before the world's racial reckoning. You'll witness how, as a shy and dejected singer, I was able to flip the script and compete in *Canadian Idol* and then go on to record music as well as sing the national anthem on one of this country's biggest stages.

By highlighting my life's achievements so far, I'm trying to illustrate that so much is possible for you, too. And you don't have to wait to get started on any of it. You can use *The Art of Doing* to kickstart the things you've always dreamed about.

I was able to give myself the room and time to complete so many things because I embraced the principles I write about in this book. I folded *The Art of Doing* into my every day. Doing so has enabled me to live a full life and allowed me to push through my struggles.

I'm here to tell you that you too can do all the things you want, and you can achieve the dreams and goals that you feel have passed you by. The method is simple, but it's not easy. However, by following what I call the "Three Ps"—Passion, Pursuit and Productivity—you'll find yourself unblocked and prepared to master self-motivation.

A common sentiment surrounds people who dare to do "too much": it's often assumed that they lack focus or discipline. Ever heard the saying "jack of all trades, master of none"? I push back on this way of thinking. Whether your goal is to be a polymath or to achieve that one big goal you have set for yourself, you have the right to experience it all. You have permission to try, to discover, to experiment and to find the joy in the process of doing.

There is no time like the present to turn the page and pursue the future you want to live in.

PART 1
PASSION

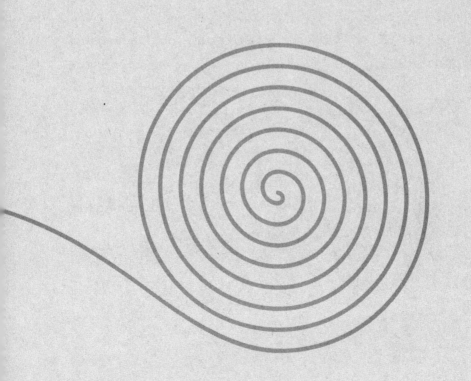

Imagine a dark, desolate, freezing-cold landscape. It's so dark that you can't see six inches in front of your face. After a few moments, you notice a fire burning in the distance. You walk to it, hoping to warm yourself. You pick up a long stick and place the tip in the flames, thinking you can use it to light a fire of your own. Once you start your fire, you fan the flames and make it as big as possible so other people can see it. Then people start coming to your fire to warm up and start a fire of their own. The fire is your passion, and this is what finding your passion and acting on it feels like. Once you find your passion, it is your responsibility to light it and to keep it burning as big and as brightly as you can.

There are other people wandering in the dark waiting for your passion to ignite.

Burn, baby, burn!

1

ACTION, MOVEMENT AND MOMENTUM

"My mission in life is not merely to survive,
but to thrive; and to do so with some passion,
some compassion, some humor, and some style."
—MAYA ANGELOU

I t is far too easy to stall our own progress by convincing ourselves that our projects or dreams can wait. Once we have convinced ourselves to set aside one dream, it becomes easier to do the same with subsequent dreams. On top of that, once we've gotten really good at telling ourselves that we can't do something, we get really good at justifying those decisions by reminding others in our circle—partners, children, friends or colleagues—why they can't either. We can even find ourselves doubling down on why we continually put ourselves second, or third or sometimes last. The truth is that we get really good at what we do the most, so we have to be very careful we don't sink into negative habits.

"How you do anything is how you do everything."
—MARTHA BECK

I can't remember where I first heard this quote or who may have said it to me, but I do know it's had an impact on how I've lived my life since.

So what does it mean? Think of it this way: If you look into someone's car and it's really messy, it's a pretty safe bet that their living spaces will be messy, too. Similarly, watching how someone treats a stranger can tell you a lot about how that person respects and feels about people in general. *How you do anything is how you do everything* reminds me to take pride in all the things—the steps, the journey, the people I may meet along the way. Everything we do, big and small, is a reflection of how we interact with our environment. Action is an important first step on the way to enjoying the fruits of momentum; however, doing it with intention is paramount. The intentions behind our actions act like seasoning when preparing a meal. Chicken is chicken, but I'll choose jerk, curry or tandoori over a plain boiled breast any day.

||||||

WHETHER YOU'RE TENTATIVELY embarking on something new or you're still mulling over a path you've been itching to take for years, you are undoubtedly facing challenges. An emotional block—of your own making or one that may have been handed to you by a loved one projecting their fears on you—may be standing in your way to getting started. Or you may be dealing with physical or mental impediments that feel like huge weights preventing your forward movement. For some of us, the smallest of problems feel so much bigger than they really are because we have been carrying them for so long. We need to look at our problems from different perspectives. A change in vantage points may open your eyes to the multitude of possibilities in front of you.

Some years ago I went tandem bungee jumping with my wife. Well beforehand we looked into the adventure company to make sure everything was as safe as it could be. Once we were satisfied with our research, we booked our jump. When the day arrived, we were excited and a little bit nervous. We got harnessed up and in position. Neither of us had done it before, and as we inched closer to the edge I felt like I needed to put on a brave face and convince my partner that everything would be okay.

With our legs tied together and our bodies fastened tightly to the apparatus, all we needed to do was jump. I was scared, but I felt my partner was a little more scared, so I acted like I wasn't. I knew from experience that sometimes all we have to do is convince ourselves that we are exactly where we are supposed to be in order to act.

The point of no return hit when we began tipping forward. No matter how hard I tried, no matter how fearful I was, I couldn't stop what was happening. That's when the most beautiful thing happened: bliss. Once we made the leap, any fear or negativity we'd felt was completely blown away. We were locked together and locked into a future we'd both agreed on. The world slowed down and we became hyper-focused on the sound of the wind, the look in each other's eyes and the feeling of surrendering to something new and amazing. Of course, once we reached the end of the cord, the G-force of the bungee was a little less than comfortable, but it didn't matter—we'd done it. Fear conquered and new lesson in hand.

Warning: Courageous steps into the unknown may produce massive feelings of ecstasy and connection.

WHILE I WAS in college, I wanted to write a musical and put it on stage. I'd never written a play, I'd never composed music, I had no experience in costume design or choreography. The only thing I knew was that I wanted to write a musical and I wanted to perform it at the legendary Martin Luther King Jr. International Chapel at Morehouse College in Atlanta, where I was a student athlete. Undaunted by my lack of experience, I didn't feel a moment of doubt or fear that my dream wouldn't come to fruition. I just kept moving forward and completing tasks. When I didn't know how to do something, I found someone who could help me make it happen. This was before Google was widely used and YouTube was created. I had to connect with real people to source what I didn't have.

I wrote my script, *The West End Story,* and then moved on to the songs. As you may have guessed by the title, *The West End Story* was loosely based on the hit musical *West Side Story*. My musical revolved around the struggles for turf and love between two rival groups. I made a bold choice with the Smokes, one of the rival groups. They were a group of White misfits, and the Black actors performed in "whiteface" as a statement about the extreme racism of the 1800s and early 1900s. When it came to the music, I found someone who could play piano, and together we composed the soundtrack. We crafted melodies and harmonies for our songs. This was my first stab at song writing, and I fell in love with it. The process of sitting, thinking, feeling and then writing down words and humming melodies was transcendent.

Next, I held auditions. Sitting in the director/producer chair and watching hopefuls line up to be a part of my show felt special. Experiencing the joy of your art through other people's eyes, mouths and hearts is amazing. My favourite part was listening to those who were casted sing what I had imagined just months before.

Around the same time, I partnered with a friend who had experience choreographing dance. I knew what I wanted to see but not what the moves were called. I attempted to show him and even made vocalizations to emphasize the intensity I wanted an arm to reach or a kick to pop. Luckily, he spoke my language and was able to translate my vision into technical directions for the dancers. Then it was time to make the costumes. My girlfriend and I paired our elementary sewing skills with consignment-store finds to complete the production.

During the entire pre-production period, I worked on getting permission to perform my musical at King Chapel. The paperwork came through at the eleventh hour.

It wasn't until I reflected on this experience that I realized the entire undertaking only happened because of *action, movement* and *momentum*. I never slowed down enough to realize that what I was doing was highly improbable. I don't even remember if the show was any good. And now that doesn't even matter. The only thing that really matters is that I took action and started the journey. My actions led to movement, and that movement led to momentum. Once you get momentum, you've already solved most of the equation. You simply need to hang on and ride it the rest of the way.

QUENTIN TARANTINO ONCE said that a director doesn't need to know how to shoot a film or light a set. They don't need to know how to do anything except actualize their vision. If you have a vision and you can articulate it to the correct people, you'll be a great director.

In many cases, we let our doubts, lack of experience and limited knowledge dictate the feasibility of our dreams. We submit to where we are rather than dream of where we could be. Quentin's take on directing reminds us to focus on what we do know: our vision.

Ensure that you can clearly articulate your vision, locate the areas in which you need expertise and then move in that direction. Let momentum fuel you rather than allow the lack of something to stall it.

If you opt out of something you want to do because you don't know how to do it, you're taking the easy way out. There are too many tools, right at our fingertips, that can help us learn how to do things and solve most of our problems. Of course there are times when it's okay to opt out, especially when your vision is fuzzy. But before you throw in the towel, ask yourself, "Is this endeavour one I really want to undertake?"

Here's an example I think many people can relate to: You hear people sharing stories about their invigorating morning runs, and it stirs something in you. You decide you'd like to be an early-morning jogger, too. You start, you fail, and then you get down on yourself and wonder why you can't do it. An honest look at yourself might uncover that you actually never wanted to be an early-morning cardio machine. Instead, it was *the idea* of that kind of life that intrigued you, not the actual living of it. A lot of people get hung up on becoming "that kind of person" instead of focusing on what's really important to them. Once you discover what you really want to do, all you have to do is act. A little bit of action creates a little bit of movement, which will kickstart the momentum you'll need to help you overcome all of the challenges that will arise along the way. Trust yourself and follow the feeling of excitement that brought you to this place. You don't need to know everything before you begin, but you do have to start in order to find out how you'll get there.

Action.

Movement.

Momentum.

2

RUN TOWARD LOVE

*"It is so liberating to really know what I want,
what truly makes me happy, what I will not
tolerate. I have learned that it is no one
else's job to take care of me but me."*
—BEYONCÉ KNOWLES

I t was 2007 and a typical hot summer's day in Edmonton, Alberta. Linda, my track-and-field coach, and I were training hard to take my high jump to the next level. I was fresh off a couple of international wins on the circuit. We were on the cusp of achieving the Olympic qualifying standard for the men's high jump. It seemed that all of my life's training, hard work and focus were aligned, and I was ready to test my abilities against the best in the world.

My training that day was to consist of some short sprint intervals, plyometric jumps and a little pick-up basketball. Near the midpoint of my workout, however, I felt an unusual pressure in the back of my head. Headaches were not uncommon for me, but this one was different and troubling. It felt as though a weight was pressing my head forward and forcing my body to the ground. It wasn't so much painful as it was disorienting. It was interfering with my regular motor functions. I remember taking an Iron Man (a.k.a. Tony Stark) knee before attempting to stand up. I couldn't get my bearings. The connection between my brain and right leg was short-circuiting. I recall looking up at my partner, who was watching with concern, and asking her if my eye was open—all I could see out of my right eye was a solar eclipse. As the vision in my right eye darkened, I tried to repeat the question "Is my eye open?" But this time my words were garbled and indistinct. What happened next is a blur.

I was rushed to the emergency room. I remember hearing nurses yell "hypertensive male . . . immediately . . ." The staff were concerned that I was suffering a stroke. After a spinal tap, MRI and many hours, my head started to clear. Unfortunately, the doctors couldn't explain why this had happened; they only knew I was out of danger at that moment. I was diagnosed with a TIA—a transient ischemic attack, which is essentially a temporary blockage of blood flow to the brain. I was released from the hospital with a lot of questions that needed answering.

I visited a neurosurgeon and my family doctor, and neither of them could give me any concrete answers either. After doing due diligence to rule out any immediate danger, I was eager to get back to training. However, my team—my technical coach, weightlifting coach, and sports medic—decided it was too dangerous for me to continue. They refused to take part in any training that might cause more damage to my body. I, however, wasn't willing to throw in the towel. Stubborn as always, I decided to train alone. I believed I could do it without their assistance, that I could manage the work and focus necessary to get to where I needed to be.

I found out rather quickly that I was wrong.

After some deep reflection and discussions with my circle, I concluded that my professional sporting career was over. It had all happened so quickly that I never had a chance to be scared. When I was going through my medical crisis, it never crossed my mind that I would never compete again. I just assumed it would work out, that I would get through it and be back on the track in no time.

Little did I know that pivotal moment would release me to live my most authentic life. A life focused on moving toward love, not running from fear.

Let me rewind a bit in an attempt to explain how I got there. After graduating from Morehouse College in 2002, I thought I was done with track and field. Up to that point, my athletic career had been decent. I'd won a couple of national high jump and NCAA championships, as well as a handful of All-American Awards, and had set countless records in my home province of Alberta (some of which are still standing). A photo of me had been featured and I was mentioned in the August 1997 edition of *Sports Illustrated* and I had been named one of Canada's top high-school dunkers by *Cage Magazine*. But the passion to wake up early every morning and get in two or three training sessions a day had disappeared. I wasn't as hungry to compete in the same way I had been when I entered the NCAA. When I'd started, I had a different vision of what my life as a student athlete would look like. I was convinced that, as a full-scholarship athlete, my journey through college would be full of fanfare and accolades. The truth of the matter was that post-secondary education was challenging. Attempting a double major in psychology and neurobiology at the same time only added to my stress. There were no easy grades, and world domination seemed distant.

I didn't make things easy for myself either. I often leaped at opportunities that excited me without grasping the toll the extra activities might have on my overall well-being. I was already a student and a full-scholarship athlete, so why not get into business, too? I trained in the early evenings and mornings, went to classes throughout the day, and on Thursday through Sunday I ran a live music venue called The Velvet Underground at night.

On paper it all felt right, but the grind of being a student athlete who was expected to keep his grade point above a 3.0 in order to retain his scholarship while competing at a high level, while also juggling life as a budding entrepreneur, took a real toll on me. I was wearing myself pretty thin and was struggling on many fronts.

I had hoped to attend the Sydney Summer Olympic Games while I was in college and to win the NCAA championship title during my freshman year. Neither of those goals were met. By the time I graduated, I hadn't achieved what I'd set out to do. I had assumed that I would have a professional track career waiting for me, but that wasn't the case. I was at a crossroads. With some of my athletic expectations falling short, I needed to re-evaluate my life. The bottom line was that I wasn't having fun anymore.

After graduating from Morehouse, I stuck around Atlanta for a while and continued to run the live music venue. I eventually flew back home to Edmonton and began considering what my next chapter would look like. My track-and-field career was, I thought, over.

As a track athlete, I'd always leaned into playing other sports and keeping busy with different activities to avoid burn- out. If I felt the long training days were taking a toll on my mental health, I would find another way to reinvigorate myself. I would play golf or basketball, draw or sing, or do anything else I thought would bring me joy and reset my brain and body. That way when I returned to track and field it would feel new again.

These distractions gave me quick hits of dopamine and helped me escape the monotony that came with doing any one thing day-in and day-out. I tended to lose interest in an activity if it was the sole object of my focus. Some might say I was running from the fear of hard work or consistency. I felt I was running toward the things I loved and trusting that everything would become more clear as a result.

(A small aside about dopamine: I find that picking an activity that excites you or brings you the most joy puts you in the best position to get the job done. However, it's best to start with your least-favourite task within that activity. That way, you can apply the positive energy and motivation you start with to do the things you enjoy the least. By the time you arrive at the fun parts, you won't need to push through as much as you would if you did it in the reverse order.)

Those who know me well don't bat an eye when I say that *Canadian Idol* was the catalyst for me getting back into track and field and pivoting my focus toward love and away from fear.

I have always been an artist trapped in a jock's body. I played all the sports growing up, but I longed for the story, the drama, the art of it all. My sister and I would choreograph dance routines and perform them for our family any chance we could get. I used to tell my mother that I would give up all my athletic talents to be able to sing like Luther Vandross. As a family, we watched every season of *American Idol*. We couldn't vote from Canada, but we'd have family betting pools and discuss our approach if ever given the chance to get on stage.

My chance arrived in 2006.

Canadian Idol, Season Four, was holding auditions, and I could hear that stage calling out to me. With a lot of help from my support circle, I obliged. "Lips" (my high-school nickname and the moniker I decided to offer to the producers during my audition) was going to sing his heart out for the judges.

In *American Idol* lucky contestants are offered a golden ticket and an invitation to Hollywood. Canada's version sent their hopefuls to Toronto. It's common for the show to shoot behind-the-scenes content of select contestants in their hometown, and they chose to shoot some of mine. It featured some of my entre-preneurial projects, some clips of me slam-dunking a basketball, and me practising the sport I had given up on, the high jump. I pushed back several times when I was asked to dust off the spikes and get out on the track so they could record me jump-ing. I really didn't want to shine a light on something that I'd left in my past. I wanted to move forward. I wanted to be more than "former athlete Jesse Lipscombe." In the end, they convinced me to do a few jumps so they could include it in the promo pack.

Once I'd agreed to jump, something inside me shifted. I didn't feel the way I had expected. I didn't feel the same pres-sure I had in the past—I felt freer. I wasn't jumping out of obli-gation. I was doing it for fun. I wasn't trying to compete nor was I trying to win. I was, simply, showing off and doing something I loved. They wanted to see me jump, and I showed them how high I could do it. I wasn't jumping with a specific goal in mind. I was purely in the moment and soaking up all it had to offer. It reminded me of when I was nine years old, just starting out in track and field. Back when high jump and all the other sports I had competed in were just an extension of playtime. Breaking a record on the high-jump apron was no more significant than doing cartwheels in the grass. I had energy, I liked jumping and I loved the feeling I got when people saw me do it really well. I was back in the same mindset I had when I first fell in love with the sport, and it felt great. I found the joy. *I followed the love.*

Surprisingly, the thing I had decided to quit, the thing I wasn't enjoying anymore, turned into something I loved once more. I realized that when I was pushing back against jumping,

I was really pushing back against time and purpose. I had been spreading myself so thin with other activities and responsibilities that I was robbing myself of the ability to enjoy the sport. In the process, I was letting myself as well as other people down. I also had the nagging suspicion that I wasn't doing my best, that I hadn't put all I could into it, and that was a hard pill for me to swallow. I'd needed a timeout. I'd needed to hit the reset button.

After *Canadian Idol* reminded me of my love for the sport, I reached out to my former coach and we discussed making a comeback. We talked about what we might have left on the table and what our approach would be this time around. The biggest difference was my commitment to myself. We both agreed that we owed it to ourselves to put everything into this comeback because we loved the sport. We loved trying to solve problems and achieve better results. We knew that prize money, medals and accolades would follow, but they weren't the focus—my love of the sport was, and we planned to do everything we could to honour that. We both knew that I had unfulfilled potential and that, under the right circumstances, I could compete with the top athletes on the planet.

My choice to compete again was met with support from those in my closest circles. They too knew that I had more to offer the sport, and many of my friends were glad to see that I'd recognized it as well. I also think they knew I could never be forced back into the sport if my heart wasn't in it.

When I returned to high jumping, I felt reborn and refreshed. I wasn't carrying any baggage. My love for the sport was the only thing fuelling my drive—and it was more than enough.

My coach and I were working harder than ever and reaping the benefits. After a few stellar competitions I became a sponsored athlete (Reebok), competing with the best in the world. During this time I ranked sixth globally. Everything was going according to plan, and we were set on making the 2008 Olympics in Beijing, China.

Prior to competing in *Canadian Idol,* I'd chased success by running from fear. I had an innate fear of failing, and winning was the only thing that mattered. I wasn't winning because I wanted first place, I was winning because I was afraid to fail. But what was I even winning at? Receiving first-place medals and trophies was nice, but they never left me feeling fulfilled.

Running from fear never gave me a chance to love what I was doing. I had always compared myself to the people around me who were doing amazing things, and I noticed that many of them seemed to be winning with less. I didn't know their stories, but from where I was standing, many of them were doing extraordinary things from a less privileged place. On the other hand, I'd grown up in a middle-class neighbourhood with parents who were still together. I had the love and support of friends and family. For me, those privileges came with a heavy and unhealthy amount of self-imposed responsibility to succeed. There were also a number of high achievers in my bloodline: my CFL hall-of-fame grandfather (Rollie Miles), my celebrity musician uncle (Brett Miles) and my pioneering aviator aunt (Bessie Coleman). That all came with some weighty pressures. I internalized it all by feeling like I had to crush everything I did. Not take any time to enjoy it, but to do it, to crush it and to move on to the next thing.

I was constantly running from fear. Running from the fear of disappointing my family, friends and, most importantly, myself. I was scared at the possibility of being seen as mediocre. I was running so fast from fear that I was winning without feeling any of the rewards. Making elite sports teams, hitting qualifying standards, earning top marks in school or breaking records—all of those things were driven by a sense of duty. I met all of the accolades not with joy but with a sense of obligation.

It was during this time that I finally came to understand the importance and necessity of having a team. I realized that no matter what I was doing, it would prove more difficult if I didn't have support. In order to achieve the best version of yourself, you will need people in your corner. I am lucky enough to have been surrounded by a strong circle of love and support for most of my life. Currently, my wife, Julia, is my rock, my best friend, the yin to my yang and the person who continues to push me to be better.

And this brings us back to that fateful training day when everything changed again, when I was taken to the ER after suffering the TIA and subsequently had to retire from the sport I'd finally found joy in.

The thing about retiring from a sport when you are not a household name is that no one cares. There are no big announcements or press conferences. No retirement dinner or drinks with colleagues. I made a decision with my team, and then my sporting life slowly started to fade away. My sponsorship ended and I stopped getting shoes and clothing in the mail. I stopped being invited to track meets in faraway countries because I was no longer jumping at competitions and achieving heights that would catch the attention of event organizers. My former reality slowly lost its potency, fading away as time wore on.

When I spoke to fellow athletes who were going through a similar transition period, I realized how much their identity was wrapped up in the thing they were leaving behind. Luckily for me, I wasn't weighed down by sadness or disappointment. More than anything, I felt a sort of rebirth, and I welcomed this new chapter.

I have always been able to keep moving forward, to not dwell too long on any one thing, regardless of whether that thing was good or bad. Nothing is ever as good as it seems or as bad as it seems, so I tend to keep moving in the direction of the things I love.

Of course, it wasn't that easy. Looking back, I will admit that I did feel somewhat incomplete for a long time. Even though I competed with the best in the world on many different stages, I never got a chance at the "big dance." I would never be able to call myself an Olympian. Being on the cusp yet not being able to fulfill that Olympic dream used to bother me. But running toward the things I loved helped me frame the events of my life in a completely different light. This one chapter of my life had come to its natural closure, and I was able to accept it. If I wasn't flexible and open to new avenues, I might have gotten stuck on the single point of not competing in the Olympics. Having the ability to put everything into a task and ride it out to its unknowable and natural completion allowed so much more to enter my life. Running toward love instead of fear or an expected outcome gave me the ability to look at the entire experience through a new and exciting lens.

THIS MENTAL TRANSITION, this shift, marked the beginning of my ability to live as my authentic self. The pressures placed upon me, by myself, loosened. I was able to look back at my life and recognize that the person who most often took the lead and held the reins wasn't truly me—it was a watered-down version of myself. A "representative." It was time for me to take back control. In order for me to regain control, however, I had to come to terms with when I had started to relinquish it. And for that I had to look back at my early days.

When I was in elementary school, I was like any other child: I cherished my friends and what they thought of me. My favourite subjects were recess and gym. But when I wasn't sprinting and jumping, I was running my own mini-casino in the schoolyard. I used what my grandfather had taught me about blackjack to win the sugary snacks my mother didn't pack in my lunch. (The house always wins!)

I was really gifted at athletics, and I loved every sport. Some of my favourite memories are of winning all the red ribbons at our school track meets. I had so many of them that the little gold safety pin they gave me to keep them altogether couldn't pierce the bundle. Unfortunately, all those ribbons ended up changing the way my classmates felt about me. Not just the ribbons but my desire to win them—or at least try my hardest at everything I did.

During recess, my friends and I would play a variety of games: baseball, tackle football, jackpot and hide-and-seek (I remember hearing them yell "olly olly oxen free" when they couldn't find me—I was one heck of a hider). We also played Red Rover, a game where people hold hands and call someone over, and that person sprints as fast as they can to try to break the hand-held chain. If they can't break it, they have to join it. I always broke it. My ability to win began to alienate me from my friends. They didn't want to play with me anymore. That's when I stopped trying so hard and started losing on purpose. The fear of being alone caused me to change who I was and to dampen the essence of me. I was sure that a muted version of myself would result in acceptance and belonging. My assumption proved to be accurate. My friends returned and my fear of loneliness subsided. However, even with that worry in the rearview mirror, I felt something was missing.

This is my first memory of voluntarily allowing my representative to take the lead, but it's not the last.

Not all of the pressure to change myself came from my desire to fit in. Some came from my environment. When I was ten or eleven years old, after winning a provincial track meet that was covered by local media, I was greeted with a surprise back at school. I knew my friends didn't always love it when I did well, but I never imagined that my success in athletics would make any of my teachers feel insecure. But that's just what happened: One of my teachers decided he wanted to compete with me. *A full-grown adult called the entire school out of class and into the schoolyard to announce an impromptu jump-off with me.*

I didn't know why he wanted to compete with me, but I remember feeling off about the whole thing. I thought it was an odd reaction for a teacher, but I never shied away from a competition, so I agreed to it. He pulled the mats out and we started our competition. We began with the bar set pretty low, then I raised the bar up to a height that was challenging but doable. I cleared it with ease. The teacher, however, threw out his back on his first attempt. A couple other teachers had to help him back into the school after he lost the competition. Suffice it to say that teacher was never my number-one fan afterward.

My win in the schoolyard solidified my understanding that my shine made other people uncomfortable.

Junior high and high school weren't much different. And almost everyone was White. It's actually pretty comical when you compare the demographics of my hometown schools in St. Albert, Alberta, to that of the historically Black college and university I attended: Morehouse in Atlanta, Georgia. Only a handful of White students attended Morehouse. In St. Albert, it was the exact opposite. In the nineties, no one would ever admit there was a representation problem or that people were treated differently for the way they looked, but that's exactly what was happening. It was as if my school and my city were not being honest with themselves for a long time. As a young Black man growing up in that environment, feeling out of place both physically and emotionally checked out. However, with both the school and city under the illusion that everything was "fine," it became difficult to digest what was going on. I was always trying to find a way to fit in, to belong and to be accepted in a place that didn't cater to someone like me. Contrary to what I had experienced in my elementary years, in high school, being an exceptional athlete was the only way I could exist as my authentic self and feel safe. Everywhere else, that damned representative was there, getting stronger and bolder every day.

I started to believe it was the representative who people wanted to meet—to be friends with, to date—not the real me. When meeting new people, I would mirror their handshake or humour. While this kind of behaviour can be useful, even powerful, in some situations, it becomes problematic when you begin doing it all of the time. In some cross-cultural situations, this is described as code-switching, which is when a racialized person ditches their colloquial ways of speaking and adopts a "Whiter" vernacular when around White people.

I didn't immediately understand how much power there was in giving my representative the pink slip. It happened, slowly and steadily, by paying attention to moments when I felt that version of me wanted to show up. I would ask myself questions like "Why doesn't the authentic version of myself feel safe in this environment?" or "What am I trying to hide?"

Once I stopped running in fear of those external influences and started running toward love, started acting as my full authentic self, it was amazing. I wasn't scared anymore.

When you run from fear—from judgment, from expectations,

from hard work or from truths you are not ready to face—you can't live in the place you are supposed to be. Once you understand that and decide to live authentically as the person you truly are, you are in a position to realign yourself and the direction you choose to run. When you are no longer trying to be someone you're not, when you refrain from comparing yourself to other people, and when you stop putting other people's dreams and desires ahead of your own, the direction you need to head in becomes very clear. Everything you were afraid of, all the people you were worried about disappointing, take a back seat, and you are left with yourself. You are left knowing that there is only one direction you can run, and that is toward love.

Fear has a place in our lives, for sure, but we give it too much power in our day-to-day activities. If, say, you are being chased by a moose, being afraid is key. You should run and find safety. (If you have never seen the size of a moose or how fast they can run, I encourage you to look it up. You'll soon understand why fear is important when dealing with these giants.) Fear keeps us alive in many circumstances; it tells us to stay clear of dangerous situations. However, sometimes we let fear lead the charge in everyday situations it has no business being in, like public speaking, cutting our hair, speaking our mind, asking for what we need, or taking the lead. We can start to believe that our fears are real when they are not. When fear stops us from enjoying the things we like, from pursuing our dreams, then it's a problem we need to address.

The life you want is and always has been at your fingertips.

We are all creators. Sometimes this term is reserved for artists, social media influencers or chefs. When we break it down, creating is the very thing all of us are designed to do. We create dinner out of leftovers, we create outfits from the clothes in our closet, we create excuses to miss appointments we don't want to attend, and we create reasons why we can or can't achieve something. Creating is at the heart of everything we are. Some of us tap into our creativity more than others, but we all have the ability to create something. And this also applies to our life: We have to decide what kind of life we want to lead and create it!

WHEN I CONSIDER the phrase "the life we want to lead," I notice it contains something very important—the word "lead." Not the life we want to follow, but lead. Leadership requires us to be active participants in the direction we want to go. Passive leaders rarely make good ones.

When it comes to leadership, fear can really muddy the waters. You can't lead from fear or, at least, you can't do it well. Perhaps you have paid your dues and are now in a position of leadership. Fear creeps in and tells you not to mess it up. During your ascension, you may have had all kinds of ideas to make the workplace better for yourself and your colleagues, but now that you are in a place to make those changes you are clamming up in fear of rejection and losing what you worked so hard for. The best leaders reject that fear. They feel fear but also know that it is coming from a place of insecurity that isn't warranted. They aren't afraid to fire people when they know they are toxic to the workplace. They understand the importance of quality hires and will put the time in to ensure their teams are getting better by the day. They stick their necks out and act on things in the moment without worrying that people may not like them for their choices. Effective leaders are brave and courageous and understand that their fearlessness is often the thing that got them to where they are now.

Many people find themselves in a place where their career has been taken from them for one reason or another. They enter a transitional period that can feel scary. Having your identity so tightly wrapped around one thing and then having that thing suddenly taken from you is jarring. Adopting the practice of running toward love can make these transitions easier.

A few words of warning: When you begin to lead with love and authenticity, you must give yourself some space and grace. Depending on your age, you may have lived with your representative for decades. That person may feel more familiar than the real you. When you step into your true self, it may feel like the first time you have ever heard your own voice. Your initial reaction may be to recoil in disgust and turn the other way. I challenge you to give yourself a chance. Give yourself the opportunity to meet the real you, the authentic version that has been hiding in the shadows. Give yourself the time to form a relationship with the true you and a chance to fall in love with that person. Once you get there, many of the curveballs that life will inevitably throw your way will be much easier to catch.

|||||

EVEN THOUGH I didn't consciously decide to run toward love when faced with the end of my athletic career, it was exactly what I did. As I considered what worked for my life and what made certain things easier to deal with, I recognized that I had made a shift. When faced with a career transition, I chose to use it as an opportunity to listen to what had been burning inside me for a long time. My transition time turned out to be a beautiful and freeing stage in my life. I attribute it to being lucky enough to see the lesson in running toward love, rather than from fear. I decided very clearly that every move I made from then on would be in that direction. I didn't have to rack my brain to figure out what direction I was going to head. I had always been an artist trapped in a jock's body, and now I had the "out" to follow that urge. I leaped at it. I have no regrets about what sport offered me, and I am grateful I had the opportunity to compete at the level I did, but looking back I can see that my inner artist, my inner creator, had been trying to get out and show himself to the world.

Luckily, the authentic me was given an opportunity to shine. Let's make sure yours doesn't remain locked away, never given the chance to truly sparkle. Let's rescue your authentic self before it is too late.

3

SAY YES

*"Don't settle for average. Bring your best
to the moment. Then, whether it fails or succeeds,
at least you know you gave all you had.
We need to live the best that's in us."*
—ANGELA BASSETT

Fake it 'til you make it. Many actors (including myself) put this aphorism into play every time we're asked to do something that might be outside of our experience or comfort zone. Can you ride a horse? Drive a snowmobile? Play volleyball? Say "yes" (provided, of course, you feel you can learn how to do it in the time between getting cast and the first day of shooting).

When I was being cast for *The Drive*—a feature film about the life of John Ware, a legendary Canadian cowboy who was instrumental in the ranching industry in southern Alberta—the director of the picture, Josh Wong, asked me whether I could ride a horse.

John Ware was a larger-than-life personality, often thought of as the Jesse James of Canada—only bigger, stronger and more legendary. He was a natural with animals, horses in particular. Not only was he a major player in Black history, but he was important to all of Canada's history. I had played John Ware on stage before, and his character has always been close to my heart. His detest for fences and the feeling of being trapped, his love of exploration and his knack for beating the odds resonated with me. I was elated by the possibility of playing him in the movie so when asked if I could ride a horse, I answered with a resounding "Yes!"

After I was cast, I watched every how-to guide on horseback riding on YouTube and crossed my fingers. I'd only been on a horse a couple times before, and both times an instructor was right beside me (and we were not moving very quickly). One of those times was when I was a fourteen-year-old kid sitting next to Regina Taylor in the made-for-TV miniseries *Children of the Dust*, which also starred Sidney Poitier. If you've ever seen the movie, there's a scene where we're in a buggy being pulled by a trio of horses and there's a look of pure terror on my face—I wasn't acting.

As we began filming *The Drive*, I was worried my lack of experience on horseback would be evident. When asked if I had any questions before getting up on my horse, I responded in the humblest way I could think of: I asked them to treat me as if I had never ridden before to ensure that I did it safely. I could tell they were impressed with my willingness to pay attention to detail and not assume I knew everything about riding. After the initial tutorial my nerves settled pretty quickly, and I felt more at ease. However, there was one scene we shot in the Rocky Mountains when I felt less than comfortable. I was riding pretty close to the edge of a cliff that plummeted down several hundred feet. My heart felt as though it was beating outside of my chest. I'm pretty sure the horse felt my fear because he also tensed up when we got near the edge. Once I relaxed, loosened my grip and took a few deep breaths, I was able to calm my nerves—and the horse's—and we got the shot. Afterward I came clean with one of the ranchers about my previous riding experience. He told me that, in all honesty, he couldn't tell that I was a rookie. He had assumed I knew my way around a horse!

When I was nervous, the horse was nervous. When I was chill, the horse was chill. Once I realized that association, I was able to ride much more confidently. That lesson—that what you put out there, you get back—is something I've been able to apply to the rest of my life.

Saying *yes* is one thing, but saying it with confidence and belief? That's a whole other ball game! When you walk into any situation feeling nervous or frightened, the smallest thing will make you jump. Walking into a situation with confidence and excitement will yield a different, and far more positive, experience.

A little positive reinforcement can go a long way. The fact that the people on set continued to tell me how well I was doing (true or false, we may never know) helped boost my confidence. In turn, I was able to relax and so too was the horse. In the same vein, early negative feedback can cause a person to shy away from taking leaps or saying *yes* in the face of uncertainty. Just as easily, someone could have told me how silly I looked up there or questioned if I had ever ridden a horse, and the whole scenario might have turned out differently.

IN THE SUMMER of 2003, I was cast as James Debarge in the VH1 movie *Man in the Mirror: The Michael Jackson Story*. During a lunch break, I was sitting near a table where some of the producers were eating. Michael Frislev and Chad Oakes were among them, and they were discussing the music for the film. I overheard them talking about "penny drops" and asked them what that meant. They told me that a penny drop was when they would buy a song from an artist (for the film) for a penny with the proviso that the artist would make money on the backend through a type of residual payment. At the time, this sounded like an amazing opportunity for an emerging artist to get some exposure. They asked me if I had any music that might be suitable for the film. My answer, of course, was yes.

The reality was I did not.

I did, however, have song ideas in my head that I thought would be great for the show. I just needed the right motivation to get them out of my brain and into their hands. I told them that I didn't have my music on me at the time but that I was due back on set in a couple of weeks. To which they replied, "Great, why don't you bring us some music to listen to when you are back and we can see if any works out?"

Amazing! Not only was I acting in a film depicting the life of a pop icon, but I was being offered the chance to have my music on the soundtrack. Now I just had to write and prepare some music. The bigger problem? I had never recorded anything in a professional studio either. I wasn't even a musician. Luckily, in 2003 I wasn't expected to email some MP3s in the next hour. I had a little time. I racked my brain about who could help facilitate this task.

When I got back home, I stopped by a local track meet to catch up with some old friends, watch some events and fine-tune my own skills. The Universiade Pavilion at the University of Alberta, also known as the Butterdome, is a multipurpose arena in Edmonton that looks like a large stick of butter, hence the nickname. I was competing there when I saw an old friend, Nathan, on the track. I had just over two weeks to figure out my musical dilemma, so running into him was perfect timing. Call it kismet. I had known Nathan for a while, and on top of being an athlete, he was an amazing singer and producer. I asked if he would be interested in collaborating with me for the movie I was working on. He said *yes* and invited me to see the state-of-the-art home studio that he had just finished constructing.

When I went to tour Nathan's studio, I met his creative partner and vocalist, Steven. I told Nathan and Steven about my meeting with the producers, the penny drop and the potential opportunity. I also informed them of the looming deadline and that I already had an idea for a song. The part of the song I had prepared was a Southern-inspired rap verse. I wouldn't say I was a rapper, but I was much more confident spitting bars than I was singing melodic phrases. I performed the verse, and both Nathan and Steven agreed that it was the start of something big. We got busy in the "lab." Our chemistry was awesome; it felt like we had been working together for years. It wasn't long before Nathan's genius producing, Steven's melodies and my lyrics melded into an amazing track. And then what had started as three guys experimenting turned into a full-fledged artistic trio. We banged out three or four more tunes, gave our group the name "Jaeness" (pronounced J.N.S, a.k.a. Jesse, Nathan and Steven), and burned a CD for me to give to the producers.

It didn't take long for the producers to respond to our offering. They were just as excited about what we had made as we were, and they told us that they liked one of the songs, "Halo," the best. They requested a few minor changes to the lyrics so the song would better fit the film, changed the song title to "Busted, " and told us that they wanted to use it in the scene where the FBI cracks down on Neverland. I brought the news back to the guys, and we turned around the revised song before the deadline.

Saying *yes* opened doors I had only dreamed of standing in front of. "Busted" became Jaeness's first single and the first song of mine to appear in a movie or television show.

The next year I said *yes* to a different offer, to be assistant to a producer. At this point in my life I was saying *yes* to any acting or acting-adjacent gig that came my way. I was asked to drive a producer around and assist him with whatever he needed while he was in town producing a film. I had never been an assistant before, but I could drive and I felt like I was in decent company. On paper, it felt like a solid connection for later in life so I said *yes*.

I drove the producer to the film studio and back to set several times a day. Occasionally, we'd run for coffee or snacks or other menial errands. I recall overhearing his phone conversations with other producers and famous people, and thinking to myself that I hoped to be that connected one day. This producer was very charming, quick-witted and sure of himself—exactly what I thought a major Hollywood producer would look and act like. We talked about acting, the film business and music. I mentioned my new group, Jaeness, to him. He gave me advice on what to do whenever I got to L.A., and other bits of inside information. I had been engrossed thinking about our music, and I was over the moon that he wanted to check out some of our stuff! Our music studio was quite a distance from the production office, so it took a while to get to the suburb where it was located. When we finally arrived in front of the building, he asked me where the hell we were. "My music studio!" I responded. "I meant the film studio," he said. "But since we are here, we may as well go in." Whoops! I was a little embarrassed but also relieved he was willing to check it out. Mistake or not, I wasn't about to miss this opportunity to share what we made.

We walked in and knocked on the studio door. Both Nathan and Steven were there. I introduced them to the producer and asked them to play some of what we were working on. As they played, the producer's face lit up. He was very impressed and told us to stop the music—he was going to call Clive Davis. That's right, *the* Clive Davis! He proceeded to call Clive and then put the phone to the speaker before resuming the conversation. After the impromptu listening party, he told me that Clive loved what he'd heard and wanted us to send him a package as soon as possible (a package generally consists of a demo, some biographies, pictures and other flashy stuff to make you look cool). I shared the exciting news with Nathan and Steven, and then left to take the producer back to the production office.

Unfortunately, my views of this producer changed over the course of my time working with him. The allure of the Hollywood producer began to fade and the truth about the man began to emerge as I witnessed how he treated many of the people he interacted with. By the time my work with him was finished, he was a completely different person than I had imagined him to be. He showed himself to be an abusive, aggressive, bravado-infused, chauvinistic guy who repeatedly crossed the line with women at every turn.

I wish I'd had the courage to speak up and quit. However, at the time I was blinded by his position in the industry and seduced by the phone calls I'd overheard and that he'd made on my behalf. So, instead, I continued to drive him where he wanted to go. I laughed at his jokes, and I toed the patriarchal and sexist line for my own potential career advancement. I won't name names, but he was one of the men outed by several women during the #metoo movement.

I grappled with the question of whether I should continue working for this man, given what I had seen. Obviously my dilemma pales in comparison to that of all the women who have been cornered, propositioned or assaulted by men just like him. I can only imagine how difficult it must be to come forward and share your lived experience for fear of ridicule, backlash or negative career and life consequences. I felt similar fears, and I didn't even have a real acting career yet. On top of that, I'm an imposing man and was never in any physical danger, nor was I at any time the object of this producer's attention. Knowing what I know now, it's clear what I should have done and how I should have acted. However, back then I was without the tools to deal with it, feeling confused and helpless. I should have said something to someone when I saw what was happening. I should have put myself in the line of fire to protect those who couldn't protect themselves. I knew something was wrong—I could feel it in my gut. Witnessing a superior's misogynistic actions in real time, I froze. I didn't intervene in a meaningful way. I continued to assist him and collect my paycheques. I regret to say that the gravity of those events didn't set in until much later, after my contract had ended.

Saying *yes* to taking action is important even when it feels hard.

Saying *yes* to the feeling in your belly when you know you should speak up and say something can be difficult. But don't simply say *yes* for yourself. Say it to make the world a safer place for other people.

Lesson learned.

SOMETIMES FACTORS THAT are out of your control can sideline even the best-laid plans. Our group, Jaeness, faced some serious roadblocks. As we tried to put together the package for Clive Davis, the cracks within our team began to show. We struggled to get all of the assets together and delivered on time. Ultimately, we dropped the ball. While there were several reasons why we didn't end up getting our music into the right hands, it really boiled down to mistrust between group members and the poor communication of our expectations and fears. Unfortunately, we couldn't resolve our issues. The package was never sent and Jaeness never recorded or performed again.

I admit I have wondered "what if?" from time to time, and that's a question I've always hated. So instead of dwelling on the *whatifs?,* I choose to remember all the positives that happened because of that initial *yes* response. I cling to all of the lessons I was able to learn and the memories I was able to make and share (some with people I still know and cherish). *Yes* allowed me to walk through doors I only dreamed of approaching. *Yes* got music that I made into the ears of the Jackson camp, Clive Davis and many other movers and shakers in the industry. After all, if I could accomplish all of that, what else could saying *yes* do for me?

IN 2005, I was on the set of *The Assassination of Jesse James by the Coward Robert Ford* with Brad Pitt, Casey Affleck and some other heavy hitters. I was getting ready to play the pivotal role of "Man Walking By," or something even less memorable, when I got a call from a good friend of mine, Shannon Tyler. She was a family friend and a local radio morning-show celebrity. She called to ask me to accompany her on a work trip to New Orleans. The radio station was trying to raise the money to distribute one million teddy bears to children displaced and separated from their families as a result of Hurricane Katrina. Shannon wanted me to accompany her and her team to the South because she felt that I had a basic understanding of the area, based on my college years in Atlanta and the southeast.

I'd been thinking about all of my friends and their families affected by this hurricane. I was playing make-believe while they were dealing with life-altering realities. When news of the hurricane hit, I wanted to do more, to be able to help in some way. And now here was someone asking me to join their small radio team in New Orleans to distribute these bears to children.

I said *yes* as soon as Shannon asked, but I had to get clearance from the film producer to leave. For whatever reason, the producer did not feel that my casting as "Man Walking By" was pivotal to the film. He gave me the green light to take off on the humanitarian mission south.

All jokes aside, it isn't good practice to leave the production of a major film, regardless of the size of your role. An actor rarely has the autonomy to turn down roles or walk off a set without consequences (I obviously wasn't in a position where my name held any weight). However, sometimes instinct and timing can nudge you in a specific direction and, if you are listening, that shift in focus can change your entire life. I knew this was a *yes* I had to follow through on.

We set off on a multiday trip, driving fourteen hours a day to get to the camps that were housing displaced children. This life-changing journey culminated not only in putting smiles on many people's faces but also in me finding the woman I would eventually marry and share two children with.

When you sit inches apart in a cramped space with someone for days on end, you really get to know them. If you want to test the quality of a relationship quickly, go on a road trip together—it will expedite matters! You'll know if it's going to work within the first few days (two days of driving is like one month of courting in road-trip years). Luckily for us, it worked out pretty well.

We visited numerous shelters and delivered hundreds of teddy bears before dodging Hurricane Rita and detouring to Las Vegas. By the time we made it back home, we had decided that we loved each other and wanted to give our relationship a go. And a go we gave it. A year later we were married, and in short succession we had two children: Chile Hurricane James Lipscombe and Tripp Ryder Binary Lipscombe.

I was lucky enough to marry a woman who later became one of my closest friends. Even though our marriage eventually ended, we remain integral parts of each other's lives. Shannon, a.k.a. Twoma (second mom), plays a huge role in the life of my youngest son, Indiana George Porter Lipscombe, who I share with my current wife, Julia.

WHEN I WAS a kid, my mother would take me and my siblings to see the musicals that would pass through town. She would encourage us to learn all the songs before the performance. After curtain call, we would go home and re-enact the entire show—costumes and makeup included. For the most part, we all enjoyed these experiences. I do, however, remember a family performance of *Cats,* for which Mom painted whiskers on our faces and stuffed our upper and lower lips with tissue paper, that didn't quite have all of our buy-in. My sister and I were for it, but my older brother, who was cast as Old Deuteronomy, wasn't feeling it. (That was perfect casting by my mother, as he sat in the corner, uninterested, while my sister and I did our best.) All of this is to say that musicals and other large-scale karaoke battles were familiar territory in the Lipscombe household when I was growing up.

In late 2000 or early 2001, when I was attending Morehouse,

The Lion King: The Musical put out a call for auditions. Since the auditions were being held near campus, there weren't too many barriers for me to give it a go. Most of my close friends knew that I loved singing and musicals, so they all encouraged me to audition. In true Jesse fashion, I said *yes*. I had never auditioned for a musical before, nor did I understand what went into one of that calibre. I simply showed up just before my scheduled audition time wearing street clothes and ready to give it a shot. We were to have both a monologue and a song prepared. For my song, I had chosen "U Got It Bad" by Usher. I had selected a monologue from August Wilson's *Fences*. When I walked into the audition space, everyone else was wearing formal attire and carrying around what I later learned was sheet music. I was so green that I did not know the term for written music and I definitely did not have any on me when the pianist requested it.

When I mentioned that I had not brought any sheet music with me, I was directed to a wall that had music for a few songs posted on it and told to choose one if I wanted to continue with the process. The only song I recognized was "Somewhere Over the Rainbow" so I selected it.

I delivered the monologue without much fanfare, and then it was time for me to sing. That's when I learned there was a difference between knowing a song and being able to perform it in its original key with live accompaniment. To say I struggled would be an understatement. The song began in an octave my voice had never met. I sounded like a prepubescent boy screaming in a car with poor brakes. Afterward, I was very aware that I had not performed as well as I could have and that I had been under-prepared for an audition at that level. I expected to hear some of those same sentiments from my adjudicators. Instead, they opted to use my performance as comic relief for themselves and those in attendance. They offered that I should continue with my acting dreams but suggested that I never sing again.

I knew that I wasn't the best singer on the planet, but I really loved singing, so their words deeply hurt. I'd grown up singing with friends and family. It was something I'd always wanted to take to the next level. After the judges shared their opinions with me, I stopped. I stopped singing in public, I stopped singing in front of my family and friends, I stopped singing by myself. Their words crushed me, and I stopped singing for over seven years.

Shannon, who at that point was a long-time family friend, knew of my love of singing, and she was the one who urged me to sing again. She called it "slaying the lion" and said I needed to destroy the thing that stood in the way of doing what I loved. In my mind, *The Lion King* audition was an ugly monster that would rear its head any time I even contemplated singing again. (Years later I attempted to slay that monster by auditioning for *Canadian Idol,* but it turned out that I still had a lot of work to do...)

In 2011, I was asked to sing the national anthem at the Labour Day Classic CFL football game between the rival teams the Calgary Stampeders and the Edmonton Eskimos (now the Edmonton Elks). I said *yes* and then had to deal with the emotional aftermath.

I'd had pre-performance nerves before, but this time was different. I was terrified. The game was going to be played on the tenth anniversary of 9/11. I was going to be singing in the same stadium where my grandfather's hall-of-fame picture hung. So I decided that I would "train" at a local karaoke bar. I would go by myself, sing my song and then run to my car and shed a few tears of embarrassment. I was relentless, returning week after week—but each time I ran back to my car I'd cry a little less.

I also invested in an Emotional Freedom Techniques (EFT) coach to help me deal with some of my emotional stress around singing in public. EFT is a type of counselling intervention during which acupressure points are stimulated by tapping or rubbing while you focus on situations that represent personal fear or trauma. My EFT coach asked me to imagine the worst thing that could happen. I said it would be forgetting the lyrics in front of tens of thousands of people. He responded, "So what? What is the worst thing that could come of that?" "Humiliation, embarrassment, and a few other fleeting emotions," I responded. In the end, I became at peace with the notion that I would experience much more negative feelings from backing out of the opportunity than I would by falling on my face in my attempt.

Weeks later, I walked out onto the field in front of a sold-out crowd of over 60,000 people. The announcer handed me the mic at the fifty-yard line and the music began. My worst nightmare was coming true: I could not remember the lyrics to the national anthem of my own country. I thought about reaching into my pocket to Google them on my phone, but I didn't have enough time. I took a deep breath, opened my mouth and, somehow, the words found their way to my lips. Crisis averted! I sang the anthem without anyone knowing the hell I had put myself through prior to that moment.

Saying *yes* to that opportunity was one of the most nerve-wracking things I'd ever done. But saying *yes* opened up a brand-new world for me, a world previously seen only in my daydreams. Saying *yes* can lead to a lot of things. The only thing saying *yes* won't do for you is keep you in the same place you were in yesterday. *Yes* has the power to effect change, and sometimes that's all we need to kickstart a passion. It allowed me to create an R&B/hip-hop group, to sing national anthems at CFL football games, to front two live funk-jazz bands (Retrofitz and Cornbread), to have my music appear in two feature films, and to perform in the musical *The Color Purple* and other award-winning productions.

Singing that anthem put things into perspective and showed me that sometimes destinations that seem out of reach are actually within my grasp. Sometimes the things we are looking at are closer than we think. When we make a habit of saying *yes*, the world nods in approval by offering us something new—a new opportunity, a new perspective or a key to unlock a door that has previously been locked within us. *Yes*. Such a small word with such enormous possibilities.

Which lion in your life do you need to slay? So often our hesitation to say *yes* to a new challenge or opportunity is rooted in fear. We attach so much fear to the unknown and worry about the potential negative outcomes of trying something new. We give so much weight to events in our past, but we don't give the same amount of weight to the possibilities in the future. We all have lions standing in our way. Now, if those lions were real, then our fear would serve a purpose, but in most cases they are imaginary. They are feelings that we didn't like and we don't want to feel again. We are so scared of our lion that we let it steal the joy from everything that comes after it.

Find your lion. Take the time to ask yourself what really frightens you. Locate it and slay it. Find the courage to roar in its face, "Not this time, big kitty. Not this time." If not only for yourself, slay it for those who are watching you. Show them it's possible to be brave in the face of fear. Let them know that even though the fearful feelings are very real, they do not have permission to rob you of the future you know you deserve.

CONSIDER WHAT SAYING *yes* can do for you. We become so accustomed to our routines and our comfort zone that it can feel like there is no time to say *yes* to something new, that it would just be too much.

Even for a day, what would happen if you said *yes* to all of the opportunities that fell on your lap? Maybe you'll run into an old friend and they'll ask you to grab a cup of coffee with them to catch up. Maybe your boss will ask you to take on a new responsibility. Or maybe your partner will suggest you both take an impromptu vacation.

Regardless of what the new thing is, saying *yes* will always open new doors and provide new opportunities for you to really live your life.

Yes.

4

BREAK OUT OF
YOUR SHELL

"Dreams are lovely. But they are just dreams.
Fleeting, ephemeral, pretty. But dreams
do not come true just because you dream them.
It's hard work that makes things happen.
It's hard work that creates change."

—SHONDA RHIMES

D o you know how lobsters grow? They moult. Once their body outgrows its shell, they ditch their exoskeleton and grow a larger one. While their new shell is hardening (it can take up to a month), they are vulnerable to their environment. Lobsters can shed their exoskeletons up to twenty-five times in their lifetime so they kinda get used to being vulnerable. For most humans, however, being vulnerable is a lot harder.

Unfortunately, vulnerability has so many negative connotations, the most common being weakness. When I was growing up, living in a world full of toxic masculinity, allowing yourself to be vulnerable was rarely encouraged. Strong men weren't vulnerable. Thankfully, these days we're starting to view vulnerability differently. I like to reframe it, to swap out the word "vulnerable" with "available." When we open up and make ourselves available to feel we can experience more of what life has to offer us.

We can use that same strategy—reframing—when we feel like it's time to grow, to ditch whatever is currently holding us back from what we know is waiting for us. Sometimes, simply reframing a word or outlook can help us narrow our focus, hone in on the passion we have for something, and make it easier for us to take meaningful steps to follow it through.

Just the thought of stepping out of our comfort zone and into the world of the unknown can stir up a lot of anxiety inside us. Every time I find myself making a leap, I feel anxious—those feelings never go away. But I have gotten better at dealing with anxiety and pushing forward.

I get a lot of my strength from my family. I think about all of the unknowns and scary environments those who came before me had to endure for me to be where I am now, and things just don't seem so hard. I am grateful to have shared some conversations with my parents and grandparents so that I have a good idea of the "shells" they had to discard in their lifetimes.

My grandfather, Rollie Miles, shared a lot with me. He was beloved by so many and is remembered by an entire city and beyond. He was an amazing track-and-field athlete, a professional baseball player and a hall-of-fame CFL football player. He was born in Washington, D.C., and attended St. Augustine's College in Raleigh, North Carolina (a historically Black college and university). Like a lobster, he had to ditch his shell. New and exciting opportunities took him from the United States to Saskatchewan to play professional baseball. Baseball was his sport of choice before Annis Stukus, the famous coach, convinced him to play football for the Edmonton Eskimos (now the Edmonton Elks). I've always considered my grandfather the original two-sport athlete (like superstars Bo Jackson and Deion Sanders, who played professional baseball and football at the same time, setting them above the rest). My grandfather was touted as one of the most versatile football players in the league and was voted one of the top fifty players of the modern era, winning three Grey Cups in a row in the mid 1950s. Rollie and his wife—my grandmother, Dr. Marianne Miles—moved to Edmonton for his career, but it was GG (what my family still calls the late Marianne—GG because she was a great-grandma to so many) who always impressed me. She was a Black woman in the fifties, living in a city steeped in its racist ways. Being a Black woman during this time was difficult on its own, but GG dealt with that and more, getting her PhD and becoming the president of the Alberta Psychology Association.

Both Football Grandpa (what the great-grandkids call Rollie) and GG were royalty in Edmonton. If any famous Black folks came to the city, my grandparents would host them. Photos of them chilling with different celebrities hung in their home. The one of my grandfather with Muhammad Ali always blew my mind. Every time I think about it, I wish I had asked my grandfather about that day. On top of rubbing elbows with the who's who, my grandparents managed to raise seven children who all went on to do amazing things of their own. When I say that I took my grandfather's advice to heart, I mean it.

One afternoon in the summer of 1994, a year before my grandfather passed, he and I were talking about life when he asked me what I wanted to do when I grew up. I didn't have an answer at the time so he pressed a little harder and asked what would I do if I had all the money in the world—if I had already purchased every toy, every gadget, every article of clothing and gaming console? If I had already travelled the world and I had an ATM that never ran out of money? If all that were true, what would I do with my day? What would get me out of bed and put a smile on my face every day moving forward? When the question was structured that way, I responded confidently: "I want to be a professional athlete. I want to own buildings, and I want to be famous." (I later added that I wanted to be an actor—I was young at the time and fame seemed exciting when I didn't know much about it.) He told me that if I did anything else with my life, if I put my focus into other things after knowing what I really wanted, I would be doing a disservice to myself and all of humanity.

I understood this to mean that our passions and our gifts are not just for us. We are given them not only to live a full life but also to be a beacon for others looking to find their own way. When we are available and open to our passions, and courageous enough to follow through with them, we illuminate possibilities within ourselves and for others.

I have spoken with thousands of people all over the world about following their passions. After I finish a keynote at a company gala or deliver a speech at a university, I often have the most meaningful conversations about dreams and goals with the attendees. Whether it's during a question-and-answer session or part of a more laid-back chat in a hotel lobby, we always circle back to finding passion and living in that truth. And what I've noticed is that when the other person is someone who practices The Art of Doing in their own life, they rarely have any "walls up" or defensiveness when we talk. They seem to be living their best lobster life—open, vulnerable and ready to ditch their shell when the time calls for it.

These types of conversations remind me of my early days as an aspiring actor, when I took part in improv sessions and learned the *"yes and"* rule. The notion is that it is every actor's duty to make the other person look good. It is their responsibility to ensure that their scene partner's jokes land harder. *Yes and* doesn't shut things down from the start; instead it agrees and looks for ways to make things even better. When I'm talking with people who are artfully doing as a lifestyle, I find we are able to inspire and elevate each other to new insights and opportunities. On the other hand, when I chat with individuals who have not yet embraced The Art of Doing, I get the most pushback. These individuals always know the best route to a place they have never been. They give you the soundest advice for a practice they've never experienced. I've had people push back on tangible advice about how to get their music or art out into the world. They'll tell me why my advice won't work for them, and then they'll create a different, and unproven, path to embark on at a later time. The possibility of things not working out is often a strong enough reason to keep things the same rather than embark on a new direction they are unfamiliar with. These people will dig their heels in to protect the reality they are currently living.

If the reality you are living is serving you and you find genuine fulfillment in it, there is no need to change anything. "Keep on keepin' on," I say. However, if you are feeling the urge to stretch and grow, you need to ditch the shell you're currently residing in. It's probably getting a little too crowded in there anyway.

If I could pick my single strongest influence for being confident in the skin I am in and living my truth, I would choose my grandma. Mavis (another nickname), a.k.a. Marianne Miles, marched to the beat of her own drum regardless of what the world thought, and it was infectious. She was so at ease with who she was at the best and the worst of times. I credit her for my ability to discuss anything and everything with strangers and friends alike. She never shied away from telling us (the grandchildren) "like it was," regardless of our age. I have some very warm and funny memories of her reminding us that she and her husband needed "alone" time to do what adults do and not to bother them. She had books and dolls around the house that depicted human anatomy, and she discussed the birds and the bees as casually as if she were talking about the weather. Little did I know she was painting a very healthy picture of sexuality, freedom, and the reality that adults well into their senior years are just as horny as the young folks in the world.

My grandma was a living example of what confidence and self-acceptance really look like, but one memory always stands out. After her mastectomy, Mavis opted out of reconstructive surgery. Even though she would proudly show off her scars whenever someone asked about her surgery, she did sometimes insert silicone breast forms into the lining of her bathing suit. On one family gathering at Alberta Beach, she wanted to get my attention as I was playing in the shallow water. Instead of yelling at me, she swiftly removed one of the silicone forms from her bathing suit and tossed it at the back of my head. Not thinking twice about it, I returned the form to her and did whatever it was she wanted me to do. Moments like this painted a picture of self-love and acceptance that really stuck with me. The way my grandma dealt with her breast cancer gave me the confidence to accept and love my own body. She ingrained in me a healthy love for myself, regardless of what anyone else had to say about me. I witnessed early on that the human body will change and fail us at times, but it will always be worthy of love—and that she had solid aim for a person well into their 60s. My grandma was never afraid to push the boundaries, to adapt and change in ways that suited her life at the time. She wasn't afraid to ditch her shell when it got too small.

When you are ready to moult your shell, you will find activities and situations that will push you out of your comfort zones. You'll get in the habit of looking for things that will elicit the nervous feeling that newness brings. The more you do, the more you'll realize how capable you are. You have the ability to do *a lot*.

Many of us have never tested ourselves to see just how capable we actually are. Pushing our limits can be exciting, but "with great power comes great responsibility." In order to stay physically and mentally healthy as well as have the most impact, we also need to recognize when to say *no*.

The healthiest and most productive folks do not shy away from trying new things. They are confident in their ability to do anything they throw themselves into. They also know they do not have to do everything. They pick and choose activities and goals that best serve them—things that add to their life experience rather than take away from it. These people are known as *polymaths*.

I am a fan of the term "polymath," as "jack of all trades" makes it sound like you can't be a queen, king or ace of all trades. Critics, however, believe that if you do more than one thing, you'll never be great at anything. But a polymath can be an expert at several things. In order to achieve true polymath status, however, you are going to have to turn down offers to do things you may excel at if the outcomes won't fit the big picture of your life. Saying *no* to some things doesn't mean you can't say *yes* to several others. The art is in knowing when it is time to transform, reinvent or change course while still staying true to yourself.

When I reflect on what gave me the conviction and confidence to do something when internal and external pressures were nudging me in a different direction, I think about my father, Richard Lipscombe. My father is a very patient, kind and caring man. He was never stingy with his love or expressing his care to his children. This is something for which I will be forever grateful as I try to emulate that while raising my three sons.

My father is a classically trained artist who travelled throughout Europe, studying the greats. The first job I remember him having was at a company called Reliable Printing. He was a graphic artist before the profession went digital. The warehouse he worked in always smelled of strong glue and fresh paper. I loved going there with him and playing with the typesetting equipment, the giant blade cutters and the darkroom, where photos used to be developed. When technology eventually did away with manual graphic design, he and my mother adapted by going into business for themselves. They started a graphic design company called Monard Graphics. He worked there for many years before transitioning to a printing company, where he stayed until his retirement. Regardless of where he worked, my father continued to paint and create beautiful works of art. He is still a sought-after artist, and his work is currently being juried at the Art Gallery of Alberta. At any point in his career, my father could have given in to financial pressures and pursued a different job, but he knew what he loved and followed his passions as an artist. To this day, my dad understands what kind of activities, influences and work fit into his life. He's never shy about saying *no* to the things that do not.

||||||

WHEN ON THE speaker's circuit, I find myself in several cities a week presenting to a variety of companies and educational institutions. Though the topics inevitably vary, I do have a few exercises I love to engage people in whenever there's an opportunity to dig in with a workshop. One of my favourites is called "The Business of Life." In the exercise, I ask each participant to imagine their life as a business. In my example, I name my business Jesse Lipscombe Incorporated. I then work through the very basic stages of creating a business plan. I write a mission statement for my life. I list my values. I even go through a S.W.O.T. (strengths, weaknesses, opportunities and threats) analysis. The point of the exercise is to determine what you want from a bird's-eye view and then ensure that everything you do moving forward is good for the business (your life). Here is an excerpt from my Business of Life plan:

JESSE LIPSCOMBE INC.

Mission Statement: *To connect with humans in true and meaningful ways and to create art in any and every way that I am inspired to.*

Core Values: *G.L.A.C.E.*—Grace, Love, Authenticity, Creativity and Energy*

* I love using acronyms to help me remember my core values.

S.W.O.T. Analysis:

Strengths: *Optimistic, Risk-taker, Patient, Forgiving, Competitive*

Weaknesses: *Disorganized, Procrastinator, Inconsistent, Impulsive*

Opportunities: *Leading groups, Inspiring/motivat-
ing, Big-picture planning*

Threats: *Mundane/repetitive tasks, Solitary work
environments, Too much rope*

This type of life plan helps you stay focused on what is important to you so you don't get distracted by something shiny and new. Don't get me wrong, I love shiny and new—just not at the expense of my priorities. As new opportunities come into your life, you can refer back to your plan and decide if pursuing the opportunity is actually in the best interest of your business or if it is more of a distraction.

I use this simple exercise to view my life objectively, to make decisions that are clearly focused on what I want and not merely influenced by things I know I can do. My Jesse Lipscombe incorporation definitely kept me on track whenever "carrots" were dangled in front of my face. It's important to note that even when you use this exercise and determine activities that fit into your overall plan, you may need to make some hard decisions when you get near the finish line.

One thing that is very important to my family is trying our hardest at anything we do. Specifically, if we say we are gonna do something, we gotta follow through. This bit me in the butt when I was watching bobsledding on TV with my kids. I don't recall whether I told my sons that I could bob-sled or if they asked me if I could and I responded in the affirmative. Either way, I said I could do it and they held me to it.

Shortly after that conversation, I Googled "how to make the Canadian bobsled team." I was directed to Bobsleigh Canada Skeleton, where I read about upcoming recruitment camps. As luck would have it, they were holding a camp in my city in two weeks. It was definitely not enough time to train properly but also not far enough away to get me off the hook. I signed up for the camp and competed for a spot on the team.

The initial testing was relatively easy for me: standing long jump, underhand forward throw and a sprint. I did well enough to be invited to the Olympic training centre in Calgary, Alberta. There, participants were further tested and learned how to push the sled, among many other skills. To avoid going too far down the winter Olympics rabbit hole, I'll just say that my days of amateur athletics and fighting for funding to send myself to competitions all over the world were behind me— especially since my wife had recently been laid off from her journalist job at the *Edmonton Journal* and was pregnant. Sure, it was great to find out that I could still compete at a high level and that, with time and practice, I could push with some of the best in our country. It was also very clear, very early, that this sport wasn't something I had the prerequisite amount of passion to explore. This experiment ended after a couple of camps in Calgary. I left knowing all I needed to know: I could, but I didn't have to.

LEARNING TO MOULT my shell and to be open to what life has to offer me has proven to be one of the best life lessons. It just keeps giving. No matter where I go, no matter how comfortable I become in my exoskeleton, I know I can always ditch it and grow a new one. The fear that used to drive hesitation no longer has any power in my life. In fact, I now look for that scary feeling. I search for ways to push myself out of my comfort zones— as long as they fit into my life's business plan.

5
LOOK UP

*"You wanna fly, you got to give up the shit
that weighs you down."*
—TONI MORRISON

My family likes to spend time at my wife's childhood home in Deep River, Ontario, as often as we can. We try to get there at least once a year, either for the winter holidays or to soak up the summer sun on the beautiful beaches the town has to offer. I actually wrote this chapter days before a Christmas in Deep (what all 4,000 locals call the place). The Wi-Fi is dependably crappy, and if I ever need to send a file of any significant size I have to take my workstation to Tim Hortons. However, this lack of technology has encouraged me, and my family, to say *yes* to opportunities that might otherwise pass us by.

We love the outdoors, but I wouldn't call my side of the family outdoorsy. To be honest, my three boys and I, if given the autonomy, would park ourselves in front of a screen for the majority of the day. However, when we visit Deep, we look up. We spend hours on the beach, making sandcastles and finding shells. We hike familiar trails, searching for animals and insects. We play, we connect, and we make brand-new memories.

When I say we "look up," I'm not just referring to lifting our heads away from our digital devices. I mean we live in the moment. Without even trying, we are actively mindful of our situation, free from the shadows of yesterday or from the fears of tomorrow that can infect the choices of now. It's a way of life.

In order to look up, it helps to believe that your next move or decision will be a great one, possibly the best! For most of my life, I've believed that the next thing I try will be "the thing"—a trait that has definitely left some of my partners feeling a little frustrated and even had me questioning my own sanity at times. When I begin something, I believe with every fibre in my being that it will work out for the best. I have always had a "sword in the stone" mentality: the notion that I am special and that, if given the chance, I will be able to pull the embedded sword from the stone and prove my worth. This isn't to say I think I am better than anyone else. On the contrary. I believe that everyone has this ability deep within themselves and that believing in yourself is key to unlocking new and exciting life adventures.

I am the type of person who is always looking to the night skies in hopes of seeing a shooting star or the Northern Lights. If I am driving during the evening, I am constantly on watch for UFOs. The belief that my time will come and I'll have a close encounter consumes much of my daydreams. I believe in self-fulfilling prophecies. To put it plainly, if I think money will fall from the sky, there is a strong likelihood that I'll be looking up at the exact moment someone is hanging their laundry out to dry and a couple of toonies will fall from a pocket into my hand. (Toonies are Canadian two-dollar coins, in case you are not familiar.) Look up. You never know what a little optimism might bring into your life.

New opportunities show up in our lives all the time. Sometimes we don't see them simply because we are not looking for them. Other times we assume an opportunity isn't meant for us and so we let it pass us by, never knowing what might have come.

In 1993, my mother was scanning the classified section in the local paper when she came across an ad looking for a loud and outgoing Black teenager, fourteen or fifteen years old, to play in a television miniseries with the great Sidney Poitier. My mother could spot an opportunity when she saw one. Knowing I didn't have any interest in acting at the time, she decided to offer me an incentive. She bribed me with marbles.

It was the mid-nineties, and I loved playing marbles. A store called Elephants Never Forget, in Edmonton, had the best ones. Jumbo steelies, the mother of all marbles, were what I was after. I'd get one if my mother could hear my voice in the audition waiting room. She wanted to ensure that I wouldn't squander this chance by being too shy or less than enthusiastic.

The marbles motivated me. My mother heard me from the waiting room, and I ended up winning the role. Who could have foreseen that a bribe would be the catalyst for my career in entertainment? I was given the opportunity to work with one of the best actors of all time. Not only that—I was to be mentored by Mr. Poitier himself. Props to my mother for looking up!

Of course, at that age I wasn't aware I was working with the first Black man to win an Academy Award. Instead, I was eating lunch with Uncle Sidney, my castmate in *Children of the Dust*, receiving advice about "the business" and life. If it weren't for television interviewers repeatedly asking me what it was like to work with a legend like Sidney Poitier, I might not have realized until much later what an honour it truly was.

The thing that still sticks with me about Sidney is his demeanour. At no point did he behave as if he were more important or more deserving than anyone else on set. He told me how hard the movie industry was but also how grateful he was to be in it. He made me believe that with hard work and dedication, a career in acting could be my reality, too. He impressed upon me that acting was a business, just like any other, that requires a lot of you if you want to get a lot from it. He also reminded me that the business was much harder for a Black man and that overcoming that hurdle would always be up to me. His advice has always stayed with me, and it's part of what helped get me through when the world was forced to stop.

At the start of the COVID-19 pandemic, the entire entertainment industry was forced to shut down. Many of us were gifted with a big chunk of time, and we had to decide whether we should look up or down. At the onset, I felt fear, sadness and doubt over the future of my career. Like many others, I was on a big show, and we received the news that we were stopping with no promise that we would return. I allowed myself to sit in those emotions for a day or two. Then I decided to lift my head up and look for the opportunities created by this new challenge.

I decided to try something new, something I later dubbed "remote-content directing" or RCD. RCD was the practice of directing a number of actors in different cities all over the world via technology. I wrote a pilot script for a limited series and got to work trying to bring it to life. One of the positive things about quarantine was that no one could tell me they were busy on another project—there were no other entertainment projects! I shared my script with several actors and crew members I had worked with in the past and asked if they'd like to be a part of my project. Maybe out of pure boredom or possibly because they enjoyed my script, many of them jumped at the opportunity.

My good friend and creative partner Andrew Misle and I did the bulk of the heavy lifting, sometimes wearing five or six different hats at a time. We were limited not only by the travel restrictions but also by restrictions on how many people could be in the same room at the same time. At one point in the production of our show, *Locked in Love* (which can now be viewed for free on YouTube), only three people could be together at a time. Navigating the production of an hour-length episodic show with over ten cast members was quite a riddle to solve. It also became one of my proudest achievements in the last decade. The sense of accomplishment I felt when we held our world premiere was second to none. We couldn't do it like we used to, with hundreds of people packed into a theatre followed by a meet-and-greet with drinks and snacks. We had to figure out a new way. In the end, we actually settled on an "old way": screening it for a drive-in audience on a massive outdoor screen. We sold out.

MY AUNT BESSIE Coleman was an early American civil aviator. More impressive, she was the first African American/Native American woman to hold a pilot's licence and the first Black person to receive an international pilot's licence. During an interview, Bessie's great-niece Gigi talked about how Bessie always knew there was more in store for her. Her father, a landowner, and her mother, a domestic, always encouraged her to dream and follow her passions. They didn't need to know the road before supporting her choice to walk it. At twenty-three years old, Bessie left home to live with her brothers in Chicago. By the age of twenty-eight, she'd decided to become a pilot. Whenever I hear folks talking about the stress of not knowing what direction to take in life or lamenting about not doing this or that, I think back to my great-aunt Bessie, growing up in the Jim Crow era of segregation and racism. Despite all the variables stacked up against a woman of colour who dared to dream of becoming a pilot, she did it. Her determination runs in my veins.

My father, Richard, who you may recall is an artist, was inspired to paint a portrait of Bessie after she was honoured with a U.S. postage stamp in 1995. It still hangs in my parents' home today. My father was Bessie's great-nephew, and his story is remarkable as well. Richard Lipscombe, the eldest son of Alberta (Coleman) Lipscombe, grew up in a community called Amber Valley, which was home to several hundred free African Americans who had migrated to Alberta in the early 1900s. They were fleeing the extreme racial hostility, segregation and violence, under the same Jim Crow laws, that Bessie had to overcome on her journey to greatness. The Amber Valley community shaped the lives of so many great Black Canadians, such as Violet King Henry, the first Black female attorney in Canada, and Floyd Sneed, the drummer for 60s/70s pop band Three Dog Night, who in turn paved the way for so many more to come, such as Cheryl Foggo, author, film director, playwright and leading historian on John Ware. Cheryl introduced me to the legendary John Ware and afforded me the opportunity to play several iterations of him in her plays and musicals.

When I think about what life must have been like for Black people back then, when the desire for equality, fair opportunity and basic human decency was ignored, I am moved beyond words. I am in a constant state of reverence for the strength it took for my people to look up, way up (to northern Alberta), to seek the life they knew they deserved. Against all odds, while many others chose to look down and keep down, my family fought on and demanded many of the rights that are afforded to me now.

That notion of looking up and making real moves, with no guarantee of a better or brighter future, was ever-present.

Families packed up and travelled north, by foot, or by horse and carriage, fleeing the circumstances that didn't serve them and holding steadfast in their efforts to create a new life for themselves and future generations. Their bravery created new opportunities for us all. There is no better example of how trusting a gut feeling and following through can change lives and connect people in powerful ways. Those people believed in the impossible and showed that if you keep moving and marching, you can find yourself in a better place.

I'm a living testament to that notion. I am a living example of what those who came before me fought for. For this reason, I'll never stop looking up—for myself and for those to follow.

6

FOCUS ON YOUR *WHY*

*"I truly believe that if you put your
goals in writing, speak them out loud,
and work for them, they will happen."*

—CIARA

I found myself caught up in a doping scandal by proxy. Let me start by saying that it was my error. I did not do my own due diligence before ingesting a banned substance prior to a major competition.

It was early 2007, and I was well into my track-and-field comeback. I was jumping higher and training harder than ever before. I was well aware that many athletes used performance-enhancing drugs to help them get to the next level. It wasn't something I did, nor was it something I judged too harshly. However, I am a fan of better living through science. I want to witness the amazing feats of human beings under whatever safe advancements become available. Heck, had I not been a heavy high jumper, I might have looked into using them myself. Instead, I was trying to shed excess muscle and pare my frame down to the lightest version possible.

The World Anti-Doping Agency (WADA) doesn't only screen for anabolic steroids; they have a massive book of banned substances. One of those substances was found in my urine after I participated in one of the most memorable competitions of my life.

Prior to the competition, I had some sinus issues and was taking an over-the-counter nasal decongestant with pseudoephedrine in it. Pseudoephedrine is a chemical substance that reduces swelling and helps air flow more freely. It is also a WADA-approved substance. When I arrived in Monterrey, Mexico, for an international competition, I attempted to pick up more of the medication. I could only find an over-the-counter pill that contained ephedrine, the natural source of pseudoephedrine. Without researching ephedrine, I ingested it and competed. I jumped a height of 2.27 metres and won (it was 2 centimetres off the qualifying standard I needed for the Olympic Games the following year). As it turns out, the natural source of pseudoephedrine isn't a WADA-approved substance.

Shortly after my competition, news broke that world record–holder Marion Jones had admitted to taking a banned substance. Everyone was talking about the scandal, known as BALCO, after the Bay Area Laboratory Co-operative, which provided anabolic steroids to professional athletes (BALCO had connections to many of the world's top athletes, such as Barry Bonds, Jason Giambi, Bill Romanowski and Marion Jones). A major crackdown on cheating in sport followed, and my case was tossed into the mix. As a result, I believe that I was punished more severely.

Typically, an athlete who has never suffered a doping infraction is given some grace. Especially in cases where the substance isn't on a banned list, they are often let off with a warning. I was banned for six months, all of my achievements that year were erased, and none of my prize money was granted to me. I was labelled, by some, as a cheater. It didn't matter that a nasal decongestant hadn't given me an advantage as a jumper; all that mattered was I had made an error and needed to pay the consequences. But I knew my truth, and I knew that I hadn't cheated.

In order to come back with a level head and continue my journey toward the Olympics, I had to dig deep to remember why I was there in the first place. After I took my lumps, did my "time" and got through the public backlash, I was more determined than ever to train and prove—to myself and to the world—how high I could jump.

Without a focused *why*, I might have packed it all in.

FRIEDRICH NIETZSCHE ONCE said "He who has a why can endure any how." Our *whys* become our armour when the real struggles and pitfalls come. They help keep us motivated when the initial excitement starts to wane. They fuel us so we can keep going.

As an equity, diversity and inclusivity speaker, I am constantly reminding myself of my *why*. The huge mountains of progress needed to make any real change can be overwhelming. The pushback from all sides can be very disheartening if I don't keep focused on why I started to speak out in the first place. For me, it boils down to home. Finding my home and ensuring it continues to be a safe space for me, my family, and my community became my priority.

As a result of the Transatlantic slave trade, I do not have a clear window into my past. I do not know where my people came from before they arrived in the Western hemisphere. I continue to research my origin story, but so far I have only uncovered a small portion. When people ask "Where are you from?" and I answer "Canada," they'll often ask "But where are you from-from?" I'll respond with "Edmonton" or sometimes I'll comment on their uncanny ability to pick up the suburban accent of St. Albert (the city I was raised in, just north of Edmonton). My answer never satisfies them. Of course, I know what they are really asking. However, I am a fourth-generation Canadian. More often than not, my family has lived here longer than most of the folks who ask the question. Still, the colour of my skin causes many to question my origin story.

That question—*where are you from-from?*—and how it made me feel was the impetus for me to say *yes* to speaking out.

Often I feel like I am standing on one foot while so many people around me are standing on two. They have one foot here in Canada, a place they can call home, and the other in the country their relatives emigrated from. If someone asks where they are from, it doesn't seem to bother them. However, for someone standing on one foot like me, that same question hits different. My one foot is here in Canada, the only home I know (Amber Valley, to be specific). My other foot is just dangling above a void, without a second homeland to ground it. When you are standing on one foot, it can be tough to find your balance. The thought of being pushed off the only place I call home is scary. *That* has driven my participation in the activism space and beyond. I want to help create safer spaces for everyone who calls this country home.

A lot of well-meaning and well-intentioned people enter the anti-discrimination space . . . briefly. In many cases, they find that they run out of steam or decide that it's just too much work. More often than not, the reason they can't stick it out is that they never identified their own *why*. They never asked themselves why they were in the fight. Without knowing why, it can be very easy to ditch the tough stuff—and if what you are embarking on is important, it will be littered with obstacles and frustrations. Once you identify your *why*, you'll have the fuel you need when the going gets tough.

IN AUGUST 2016, I was on the street filming a PSA about how amazing Edmonton and its transit system were when, ironically, a car full of middle-aged White men pulled up in between takes and screamed grotesque racial slurs at me. Sadly, bigoted remarks have followed me for most of my life; however, when a complete stranger yells them at you it is very jarring. I walked up to the vehicle, crouched down on my knee, opened the car door and asked the men why they had made the comments, giving them a chance to say them to my face or explain why they thought they were appropriate comments to yell at a complete stranger. Not surprisingly, they denied saying the words, slammed the door, and yelled them at me one more time as they sped off.

Luckily, the cameras were rolling the entire time and my film crew caught most of the altercation on tape. We finished shooting and then discussed what to do with the extra footage. After speaking with my wife and getting the go-ahead from the producers, I decided to share the clip on my social media accounts the following morning. We hoped to start a conversation about race and discrimination in our city and maybe get the attention of a couple of local media outlets. We ended up kickstarting a nationwide anti-discrimination movement that my wife coined #MakeItAwkward.

The days of letting destructive and damaging language and behaviour slide are long gone. The #MakeItAwkward movement encourages people to stand up, step in and disrupt these actions. When I confronted the men in the car, asking them to explain themselves, what I did was turn the tables and make the situation awkward for them.

After the video reached over a million views in forty-eight

hours, we knew we were on to something powerful. Media across the world seemed to agree—I did over seventy press interviews worldwide. Everyone was talking about it. There were times when I was doing a phone interview while my face was being splashed on three or more TV channels at a time. Most radio stations were talking about what had happened, too. A couple days after the incident, the mayor of Edmonton, Don Iveson, called to discuss what happened. We agreed to meet in his office the following day to have a frank conversation about discrimination in our city. A few other racist incidents had occurred recently, and it was painting our city in a (fairly accurate) bad light. We spoke at great length about how to address the issue—we couldn't just say we were upset and hope the problem would go away on its own. I encouraged the mayor to garner action from the city.

The #MakeItAwkward campaign, a movement focused on creating everyday activists one conversation at a time, developed three tools for dealing with discrimination of any type: 1) Why, Why, Why?, 2) The Friend Zone and 3) Get the Lettuce Out.

Why, Why, Why?

Imagine that you are at a family gathering, and your uncle or aunt begins telling a string of racist or homophobic jokes. In the past, this type of talk would garner a few uncomfortable laughs or maybe smiles from those within earshot. The "Why,

Why, Why?" tool urges you to ask the person why they feel that type of language is appropriate. It's a simple but powerful way to start a dialogue. The family member already has the floor, and your question, if asked earnestly, forces them to defend an indefensible position. Usually, they'll try to brush off their comments or claim they were just a joke. They might tell you to calm down or quit being so sensitive. Asking why again, calmly and with real interest, shows them you want to have a serious conversation and doubles down on getting them to consider why they said the words in the first place.

Any stand-up comedian will tell you that if one of their jokes bombs or lands flat, they'll probably strike it from their set. If it gets a little giggle, however, or even a glint of a chuckle, they'll keep it, believing the joke may have some legs and needs a bit of massaging before it is ready for the next gig. A person dealing out any kind of slur in social situations is no different (except, in most cases, they're not a professional comedian). Being challenged to give their reasons for telling the joke is the opposite reaction to the one they are hoping for. I wouldn't expect them to thank you for calling out their damaging words, but you will have helped to establish a new environment where that type of behaviour and language is no longer tolerated. You might be the first or the fifth person to confront the relative, but at some point, they will remove that joke from their set list and that behaviour may become a thing of the past.

The results of asking *why?* and the effects of not having a reason are very powerful.

The Friend Zone

The second #MakeItAwkward tool is "The Friend Zone." This works wonderfully in group settings like a bus or a subway, where you are the bystander watching a stranger getting verbally assaulted by a discriminatory predator. Most people try to stay out of these situations, which is understandable as personal safety must be a concern. However, this strategy urges you to focus your attention not on the attacker but on the victim. Stand or sit next to the person being harassed and tell them that the person berating them does not speak for the collective. You can assure them that they have your support. Befriend them, strike up some small talk and encourage other onlookers to do the same. Before you know it, the power dynamic will shift and the victim will be surrounded by a wall of support.

Get the Lettuce Out

The last #MakeItAwkward tool is "Get the Lettuce Out" (GTLO), which was inspired by the idea that good friends tell each other when they have something in their teeth. The same rule should apply when you inadvertently make a discriminatory remark. Maybe you thought you were making a silly joke or didn't realize the harm in your words. Regardless of the reason, a good friend should call out your error and help you correct your behaviour. Most of us would like our close pals to steer us in the right direction, but we hesitate to do the same for other people.

I have spoken at hundreds of schools over the years and a common thread among students is the importance of maintaining their social landscape. They are afraid to upset the status quo and (even though they know they shouldn't) they often choose to stay quiet when they should speak up. I tell them the same thing: GTLO. You expect your friends to do it for you, so make sure you repay the favour.

FINDING YOUR *WHY* all boils down to being honest with yourself. It's about understanding the difference between doing what you think the world wants you to do and doing what you really want to be doing (or not doing, for that matter).

It's not as easy as it sounds. In order to really get a clear picture of your motivations, you have to peel away a lot of uncomfortable layers and get real with yourself.

When I was younger, I thought I wanted to be an actor because I wanted to be famous. I thought my *why* revolved around attention, fanfare and money. At that time, a lot of my actions were centred around my ego and external validation. However, after I spent time working on myself and really digging deep into the reasons why I was chasing specific dreams, I realized that I was chasing praise and validation from the outside world. And those feelings stemmed from fear, insecurity and ego. My true *whys* became clearer the more time I spent loving and accepting myself and the less time I put into being a people-pleaser. It was almost as if I had cleaned off the lenses of my dirty sunglasses and was finally able to see what the world had to offer me.

My dreams didn't change with this new perspective, but the reason I chased them did. My desire to be an actor now was rooted in wanting to connect with people in an honest and meaningful way. I love this career because it allows me to step into a variety of shoes and live, briefly, as another person; when I do it well, I gain empathy and understanding for the world around me. My *why* now has little to do with fame and fortune, and everything to do with connection, truth and love. I would never have been able to figure that out had I not been honest with myself and made the choice to work on the less-than-ideal parts of me I uncovered in the process.

I am reminded of a speech I delivered at AMSCAR (Alberta Medical Students' Conference & Retreat) in 2013, where I reference the internal drum inside us all. I'm including a portion of my unedited speech here, both as a reminder to myself to keep living to the beat of my own drum and, hopefully, to inspire you to do the same.

Begin Standing in silence, then begin with a short, rhythmic step (***) (***)

Life without a beat
Life without a drum . . .
Is a life without direction
A confused life, or a very troubled one

You see whether the beat is innate
Or in your iPod headphones

It points you in the right direction
Some say it leads us home

It may be a drum
In this case (***) it's my foot
But really it's a metaphor for the power within
It's a guide, that's the hook

There is a pounding within us all
That attempts to lead us right
To new destinations
And to reach great heights

But we must first realize that it is there
That beat that unites us all
For once we find the rhythm within
Stand strong we can, with no fear (***)
No fear and no chance to fall

My message is simply . . . to follow your drum, your internal beat that guides you and me. It is that same beat that has me standing here today, the same beat that brought your faculty members into my life, and the same beat that had me follow it . . . dancing to that beat all the way to here . . . where I stand today.

This world is full of distractions, so many things to take your eye off the prize. Many times I have been asked what is my secret to staying focused and keeping my eye on the goal. The answer has often eluded me. How can I put something so intangible into a concise sentence? How can I try to recreate that burning beat, that internal message that has truly been my focal point throughout life to date?

It has taken me some time ... but what I have come up with is this ...

Pay attention to your internal drum and listen to your drumbeat. When you understand your real reasons for doing something, your real motivations, you'll be equipped to walk through the fires that will undoubtedly burn in your path, and you'll be able to do it with conviction and authenticity. More importantly, you'll put yourself in the best position to stay the course.

Everything is better with a beat. It's time to listen to your own.

PART 2
PURSUIT

TGIF, an acronym everyone knows, pushes us to celebrate the end of the dreaded work week and look forward to the weekend. I am a fan of TGIT: Thank God It's Today. I love putting pressure on the only thing we know we have for sure—this moment. Walking through a cemetery from time to time is a sobering but useful exercise to help us be present in our lives. Consider the dates on the headstones—birth year and death year, with a small dash inbetween. That dash represents a person's entire life: their dreams, goals, lovers, children, heartbreaks, achievements . . . It's everything. If you could fill your dash with whatever you wanted, what would you put into it? I want my dash to be filled with joy, love, laughter and risk-taking. And I'm doing everything I can to ensure that fun is slathered over everything as well. Thank God It's Today.

7

BELIEVE

*"Don't sit down and wait for the opportunities
to come. Get up and make them."*
—MADAM C.J. WALKER

What you believe about yourself is far more powerful and important than what others think about you. Let me repeat that: *What you believe about yourself is far more important than what others think about you.* In fact, what other people think about you is really none of your business. Your business is you.

In the self-help space, a lot of attention is paid to hard work and discipline. Even though they are important habits to cultivate, they're rather ineffective without belief. When we don't truly believe, deep in our subconscious, that we can achieve a certain task, it becomes very difficult to find the discipline to create hard-working habits to meet our desired outcome. We may say we want people to give us a shot, or we may attest that we deserve something, but if we don't fully believe it in our bones, how can we expect the world to?

Here's a recent example: After I participated in a panel discussion, an audience member asked me a question. They wanted advice on networking and getting noticed in the entertainment industry. They told me that they wanted to be an actor. "It starts with you," I told them. "You have to claim that space for yourself before anyone else will take a chance on you." I went on to explain that if I were casting for my next feature and I had to choose between someone who *wanted* to be an actor and someone who *was* an actor, my choice would be clear. Then I asked the person to say "I'm an actor, and I am looking to connect and network with some people in the industry," and to tell me if it felt different. I felt it, the room felt it, and the person definitely felt it. Then I asked them a more important question:Why are you so hesitant to truly believe in yourself when belief is the single most potent ingredient when it comes to actualizing the future you want?"

People serve as mirrors for us, showing us the good, the bad and everything in-between. My favourite thing about connecting with other humans is the way I see myself when I am with different people. The parts of me they bring out differs from person to person. Every new interaction I have offers me a different truth about myself.

If someone tells you something about yourself that is completely untrue, it probably isn't something you can see in a mirror and it likely won't bother you. It's very easy to dismiss a comment that has zero ounces of truth in it. For example, if someone said you were a purple butterfly, you'd probably laugh. (Unless, of course, you really are a purple butterfly.) The same holds true if someone tells you that you aren't good enough or that you can't achieve something. If you are confident that you can achieve the thing, their assertion won't pack much of a punch. It would be as if a toddler told you they could read more books than you—it might be cute to hear, but it's just not true.

I've had numerous conversations with people about why they feel they can or can't do something. Oftentimes a person can recall a moment when someone else's words planted a seed of doubt inside them that continued to grow over time. A moment when someone who meant something to them told them they couldn't. Those words become part of us. They attempt to worm their way into our identity and define us. Before we know it, we are saying the same things about ourselves, with certainty. We find ourselves shutting down potential opportunities and reaffirming limiting beliefs handed to us by someone else.

Those words don't always come from the outside, though. Sometimes it's the voice in your head telling you all the reasons why you can't do something. That voice reminds you of how you messed up in the past and how the same thing is likely to happen in the future. This negative mind chatter causes you to see every other person as more qualified than you or forces you to stay in your own lane and stick to what you know. That voice is so powerful that even when everything in us wants to believe we can, it finds a way to convince us otherwise.

When a bad thing happens, we tend to make it personal. We'll blame ourselves for the outcome even when there's no real evidence to support that we had a hand in it. In fact, we often give ourselves much more credit for causing a reaction than is justified. For example, say we notice a that a co-worker ignores us and assume we must have said or done something to cause it. We may take it a step further and assume the person doesn't like us. Once we believe that we have that power, well, the sky's the limit. Every time someone near us is in a bad mood, it must be because we are unlikeable and they detest us. We might find ourselves scrolling through a social media post, sifting through all the comments and focusing only on the negative ones. We could have received a thousand positive comments, or hundreds of great reviews, but when one or two negative ones roll in, we'll focus on them and accept them as law.

Catastrophizing—assuming the worst is always going to happen—is another type of negative thinking, and it can be very destructive. Maybe we failed to sign our child's permission form in time or we got pulled over for speeding. Someone with a catastrophizing mindset might internalize that to mean they are the worst parent alive or the worst driver ever. When I was a child and my parents were running late getting home, I used to sit at the window and think about how my life would be without them. I was sure that they had been killed in an accident and that I was going to have to deliver the eulogy at their funeral. I'd plan how I was going to tell my siblings and how we would need to divvy up the responsibilities of keeping the house together. These were the thoughts of a seven- or eight-year-old! As an adult, I've been able to manage these kinds of feelings, but they still show up from time to time. I'll notice it when I'm holding hands with my wife or one of my children while walking down the street. My mind is constantly strategizing what I need to do to ensure they are all safe in the event of a car jumping the curb, an attempted mugging, a tree falling from a lightning strike, or a meteor falling from the sky—I stay ready.

I'm sure you've heard the phrase *practice makes perfect*. Whenever my coaches said it to me, it'd go in one ear and out the other. Then someone reframed it to me as *practice makes permanent*, and that one hit home. I began to understand that I am creating patterns and solidifying neural pathways in my brain with every thought and action.

I started to be mindful of when my internal negative chatter would engage. It was surprising how often these types of thoughts circulated through my head. Once I focused my attention on those negative thoughts, I could try to replace them to diminish their power. One strategy that works well is to say the exact opposite of what you were thinking. Say it out loud, say it in your mind or write it down—whichever way feels the most comfortable to you. The key is doing it.

If you catastrophize, you've likely spent years telling

yourself you couldn't do something. Each time you practised negative self-talk, that neural pathway got stronger and stronger. Practice makes permanent. It's time to practice something that will benefit you.

When you begin flipping the negative chatter, it may feel like you are being fake or inauthentic. That's fine. Roll with it. Remember that the negative thoughts have had an enormous head start creating the grooves of lies that you hold to be true. *Fake it till you make it* has never been a more important strategy. You need to retrain your brain. Once you've gotten into the practice of identifying your negative mind chatter and proactively stating the opposite, you have to act on those new positive feelings. By identifying these key areas of focus, we can create a brand-new narrative that serves us.

I STARTED PUBLIC speaking when I was twenty years old. The first time I was asked to speak it was to graduating high-school students to offer some motivation for their future. I was so nervous I could feel my carotid artery pumping in my neck and sweat rolling down from my armpits. Twenty-four years later, I am still speaking, albeit to larger crowds and on different topics.

I am often asked if I get nervous when I am on stage. My answer hasn't changed since I spoke at that high school decades ago. I still feel the blood pumping in my chest and neck. I still feel the sweat rolling down my arms. And I still worry that my next speech might be the one that tanks and that

I'll never be asked to step on a stage again. The difference now is that I know what to expect. Every time my nerves creep in, I imagine they're like the giant curtains on a stage and I know what lies on the other side. No matter how heavy and scary the curtains are, I know there's always a feeling of accomplishment and pride on the other side. I also know that every time I shied away from parting those curtains and walking through them, I was filled with regret and disappointment. Having the tools to move through those feelings before they become cemented in my brain freed me to continue to dream and perform to the best of my abilities. I had to do more than wish the negative thoughts away or try to convince myself they weren't there. I had to embrace my emotions and believe that everything I was hoping to feel was just waiting for me on the other side of them. I couldn't just say I wanted to be a speaker, or a singer, or a comedian. I had to part those curtains and do it. I had to feel all of the fear, anxiety and panic, and then I had to learn to move through it. It was hard and it was worth it.

Of course, there were times when I almost went the other way. When I almost let my nerves stop me from achieving my goal. I made the mistake of assuming my nerves would dissipate and public speaking would get easier. Once I realized those nerves never go away, I just got better at using them to my advantage. My belief in my ability to get through acted as a propellant.

We see what we believe. One of the most important features of belief is that it is up to us to decide what to believe. If we believe something is going to be hard, rest assured it'll be difficult. If we believe someone is going to treat us poorly, we'll be able to pick something out of our interaction to support that narrative. Accept that you have the power to alter your experience with a positive mindset that supports the outcome you desire.

Once you can do that, you need to plan your path. Don't be afraid to aim high and shoot for the stars. When I was in high school and needed to keep a certain grade average in order to qualify for my post-secondary scholarship, I would hit that exact number or one percent higher almost every time. Then later, when I worked in sales, I would set a goal I believed I could hit and then meet it. Now that I'm a father, I give my sons the same type of goal to set for their grades. Just like their dad, they hit that number.

What would happen if we aimed a little higher, or believed we could do a little more? I'm confident we'd hit those targets as well. We hit them when we believe, with every fibre in our being, that we can, and then we follow up that belief with a concrete goal and align our efforts to that goal. The belief is the fuel in the car. No matter how complex your journey or how well-equipped your car, without the fuel of belief, you'll never arrive at your desired destination.

Think about a past goal you fell short of achieving. Did you truly believe it was possible? Or did falling short have more to do with your lack of belief than your lack of ability? Even though you went through the motions and put in the hard work, did you still hear that little voice in the back of your head telling you that you couldn't do it?

When our actions don't match our beliefs, when the things

we think don't match the things we say, we're putting obstacles in our own way. Once we remove negative self-talk and doubt from our mind, we can get to the doing of really big things. Once we get there, we can aim as high and as big as we want. Practice makes permanent.

8

BE THE GENIE

"You can't be hesitant about who you are."
—VIOLA DAVIS

I'm sure all of us, at some point, have fantasized about stumbling upon a genie in a bottle. I know I have. What would your three wishes be? Would you wish for a billion dollars? World peace? Good health?

If only life worked that way.

This is just another example of how we keep looking outward for ways to fulfill our dreams when we should be looking inward. You and only you are the magical vessel you need to find to achieve your goals. And the coolest part about this realization is that you're not locked into the whole three-wish paradigm. You can grant yourself as many wishes as you like. You simply need to give yourself permission to do it first.

Before you can give yourself permission, however, you need to forgive yourself.

No matter where you find yourself right now, there is a good chance you have done something you wish you could take back. Regardless of the situation, forgiving ourselves is often very difficult. We tell ourselves stories about why we are not worthy of forgiveness, why we have to hold on to guilt and shame. I still have a hard time letting myself off the hook for elements of my past, even though I know that doing so would put me in a better headspace. I struggle with the *what-ifs?* and the *maybe if I had* from time to time. Could I have worked harder as an athlete? Did I prepare as much as I should have for my audition? Might I have been a better partner and father? The answer to all of these questions is *yes*. However, worrying about and fixating on them does nothing to help me be better in the moment and tomorrow. I have to forgive myself for yesterday so I can give myself permission to thrive now.

For some of us, that's the hardest thing in the world. It has been ingrained in us from our very beginnings that we have to look externally for permission.

Parents are the first people to give us permission, and the first people we have to ask for permission when we want something. If we wanted a second helping of dinner, we had to ask. If we wanted to watch TV or stay out late, we had to ask. Learning to give ourselves permission is a process that happens as we grow. The more we practice doing it, the easier it becomes.

We live in a world that promotes hustle culture, where working every waking hour with few breaks is seen as the norm. We complain about our co-workers, our bosses, and the fact that we never have enough time off or don't get paid what we're worth. We lament that there is never enough time. What we fail to do is give ourselves permission to change it all.

I like to put it this way: A person wouldn't ask a professional hockey player how to fix their car, so why would you ask anyone else to "fix" your life? Granting ourselves permission—permission to try something new, to act differently, to change our circumstances, even to disappoint others or fail at something—is the key to being the genie of our own bottle.

WHEN WAS THE last time you danced until you were dripping in sweat? The last time you turned on some music, stood up and busted a move without worrying about what you looked like? As kids, we'd hear a beat and just move our feet. As adults, we dance a lot less frequently. Blame it on sore and achy body parts if you want, but the truth is we stop giving ourselves permission to move. It's time to dance again. Do it for no other reason than the hormones it will release and the joy it'll bring. I give myself permission to dance any and everywhere the mood strikes—and doing it publicly seems to give others permission to do the same. It's contagious. My willingness to dance has also given me some amazing opportunities that I surely wouldn't have been given if I had been a stoic wallflower.

Back in my college days at Morehouse, I found myself backup dancing for R&B singer Mya while she was on tour with

Jermaine Dupri, Busta Rhymes and a few others. The opportunity presented itself after I accepted an invitation to "dance battle" someone on stage. After confidently thrusting my body in multiple directions, I was offered the gig. Another time I was in Daegu, South Korea, when I caught wind of a dance competition where the winner would receive two round-trip airfares to anywhere in the world. I entered and won! You might assume I'm a professional dancer, but that's not the case. I'm simply confident in motion. I let my feelings take over, and I grant my body permission to move freely. Each time I really leaned into that freedom to move, amazing things have resulted. Something as simple as dancing without worry of judgment has provided me with many opportunities and memories.

Another time I participated in a fundraiser in Alberta where I was asked to have fun and show off some dance moves with other local celebrities in an improvised ballet-parody routine. We all wore ridiculous outfits. I was in bright-coloured tights and a pink tutu, and my counterparts sported their own tickle trunk–inspired wardrobes. I jumped, spun and lifted people in the air, all in the name of charity. Staff members from the Alberta Ballet School happened to be in the audience. They were so impressed with my "performance" that they later offered me a full scholarship to the Alberta Ballet School! Now, I understood that the school did not have an influx of strong, athletic men beating down their doors, and that their offer may have had more to do with my potential ability rather than my actual ballet skills; nonetheless, it was a legit offer, documented in the local papers. As honoured as I was, I declined the offer. It just wasn't in the cards for me at the time. However, granting myself permission to do something as simple as dancing opened a door I'd never even dreamed of.

What might something similar do for you?

PEOPLE OFTEN ASK me how I feel about multitasking, given that I've done so many things. They see the balls I'm keeping in the air and wonder how I do it all. What they haven't seen are all the balls that have landed on the ground. Of course there have been some casualties in my attempts to master keeping multiple projects on the go. However, the more I try new things, the easier it becomes to try more new things.

Think about it this way: If you are only holding one ball, dropping it can be devastating. However, if you live with an abundance mindset—believing that there is so much available for you—things change. Then if you are juggling more than one ball, dropping one or two is much less devastating. You still have a number of perfectly viable balls in the air. You'll be able to pick up the ones that fell on the ground and try again.

Often the words *try* and *do* are at opposite sides of the productivity table. Trying gets such a bad rap. (I blame Yoda for saying "Do or do not. There is no try.") But trying is the seed of doing. It's the first step in changing your current situation to the one you desire. The more you try, the better you will get at whatever it is you are doing and the more opportunities you will have for a positive outcome.

With every attempt you make, you will learn something that you can use the next time you try. If you don't get the outcome you want, try again but in a new way, using what you gleaned from your last attempt. I find myself modifying how I try things every day. I try differently each time, and I become more and more effective at trying. I can confidently say I am really good at trying because I gave myself the chance to get better at it.

Remember, you can try something as many times as you please. You're the genie.

In addition to trying, give yourself permission to make mistakes—both the chance to make them as well as the grace not to judge yourself harshly when you do.

I started my first company, Entrephoria, when I was a teenager. Back then I didn't know what being an entrepreneur really meant, nor did I know how to start a business. My best friend, Christine, and I just knew that we wanted to create something cool, and we gave ourselves permission to try. We saw an opportunity in the market and moved toward it with curiosity and optimism. We weren't old enough to go to nightclubs, but we did notice that most of them were only open three nights a week and seemed to sit empty otherwise. We wondered if we could utilize that space during off hours to organize our own version of *America's Got Talent*. A fun business for us and another revenue stream for the clubs. We contacted a bunch of establishments and inquired if they would entertain our idea. Many of them wouldn't give two teenagers the time of day. A couple of them, however, heard us out and agreed to let us use their space. We were thrilled. We set about advertising for talent and generating a roster of people who wanted to showcase their abilities for a shot at winning prizes or being considered for future gigs. Relatively quickly, Entrephoria evolved into a small talent agency and event company. Christine and I were being our own genies, and it paid off.

We didn't know anything about business at the time, nor did we know how to run a talent agency. We figured we could learn all of those things on the go or with some reliable tutelage. It's true that ignorance can be bliss at times—the fact that we didn't know a lot actually helped us move without fear. We learned so many valuable lessons just by simply trying without any preconceived notions of what could go wrong. We didn't wait until we had "all the information" before starting. We saw an opportunity, believed in our own abilities and made it happen.

SOCIETY PUTS A lot of pressure on us to know what we are doing with our lives. There's a lot of pressure to have our five- and ten-year plans mapped out. People expect us to know what we want to be when we grow up, when we'll get married and have kids, when we plan to retire. But it's perfectly okay not to know any of those things and not to be in a rush to find out. Actually, it's quite liberating.

Being okay with exactly where you are at any given moment is key to being able to leave that place, if you so desire. You have to know where you are to get to where you are going. If you accept that you have no idea what you are doing right now, you can give yourself the space to figure out your next steps when you are ready.

All too often we lie to ourselves and to others. We say that we have it all figured out when that's the furthest thing from the truth. While we are living that lie, we are also preventing ourselves from moving closer to where we really want to be.

Have you ever heard yourself say *I could have done that if I'd tried harder*. That, my friend, is what I call the "buffer excuse." It's a way we justify failure and half-hearted attempts. It's how we protect ourselves from disappointment. And it's the result of not giving ourselves permission to succeed. If I know I didn't put my all into something and I fall short, I can console myself that results would have been different if I'd just put in a bit more effort. However, if I tried my very best and still didn't achieve what I set out to do, well, that's an emotionally fraught place to be (and then I'd need to put in more work to forgive myself).

Granting ourselves permission to succeed means that we allow ourselves to try our hardest no matter the outcome. Once we grant ourselves permission to try our hardest, we automatically remove any chance of using the buffer excuse.

You have to get out of your own way and accept the greatness inside yourself. None of the greats throughout history were surprised by their achievements. It never came as a shock to them. They expected to be great. This doesn't mean they realized their goals without experiencing pitfalls or setbacks. On the contrary, they knew failure is part of success. Michael Jordan wasn't surprised when he became the highest-paid Nike athlete.

Steve Jobs wasn't shocked when he developed the iPhone. Prince didn't startle himself with another number-one hit. They granted themselves permission to be great early in their lives. Too often we ask ourselves *Why me?* or *Who am I to do this or that?* I say, who are you not to? Give yourself permission to be the greatest version of yourself you can imagine.

People often confuse confidence with arrogance. Confidence is rooted in self-worth and doesn't depend on external validation. Arrogance, on the other hand, stems from a lack of self-worth and a need to dominate others. Accepting your own greatness gives room for your confidence to exist. If you are filled with doubt and negative mind chatter, you won't have any room for the greatness that is knocking at the door. When you worry less about what others think of you, you'll find you have much more capacity to grow.

As Maya Angelou said, "Do the best you can until you know better. Then when you know better, do better." It's not fair to define our present selves by who we used to be and what we used to do, yet so many of us seem to be tethered to whispers of who we once were or the things we did or we experienced. Our past can certainly inform our future, but it doesn't define it. Who we were last year doesn't have to be who we are today. Whoever you used to be, whatever label you put on yourself, is not permanent. Grant yourself forgiveness for having come up short and then move forward.

You are your own genie in your own storybook. You can turn the page and begin a new chapter.

9

YOU ARE
MORE THAN ENOUGH

"The most common way people give up their
power is by thinking they don't have any."
—ALICE WALKER

f I were a little thinner, if I had more money, if I were smarter, prettier, handsome, braver, organized, disciplined ... Excuses are just reasons marinated in emotion. What if you were enough right now? What if you could just show up, without all the sauce, and accept that you are enough as you are?

You are enough right now.

Accepting you are enough is more than taking stock of all the good things in your life. It's also understanding that the bad things are essential to who you are—right now and in the future.

Both the good and the bad things you have gone through are essential to who you are as a whole person, and that whole person is more than enough.

An exercise I have done myself and encourage other people to do is to look into a mirror and say *I love you so much and I am proud of you* every night before bed. To say it and mean it is a lot harder than it sounds. When we take the time to say *I love you* to ourselves, we are often flooded with thoughts of why we shouldn't. Our mind likes to point out all the mistakes we've made during the day. Just like any practice, however, the more you do it, the easier it becomes.

When I was a young high jumper, I went through a rough time when I hated looking at myself. I actually removed the mirrors from my house. Not only did I shy away from my own reflection, I also avoided taking my shirt off in public. Keep in mind, I was a professional high jumper at the time and in the best shape of my life. I couldn't see it. All I could see was what other people told me to see. Their words shaped what I saw. Other athletes, coaches and the press had made up their minds that I was too big to be a high jumper. My coaching team would encourage me to change my diet, to get on the scale daily to track my weight loss, and then suggest other ways I could drop pounds so I could be a more efficient athlete. On paper this all made sense: I was larger than most other high jumpers, and even though I maintained less than 10 percent body fat at the time, I was still well above the average weight of my counterparts. Newspaper headlines read *Linebacker Lipscombe Too Big to Jump,* and it did a number on my self-confidence. I felt horrible about my physical appearance every waking hour. This feeling isn't foreign to many women, as society has created a beauty standard that is almost impossible to match. Less publicized, however, is that men also struggle with the external pressures to look a certain way, and I wasn't immune to these.

Now that I am decades removed from being a professional athlete, one of my most powerful takeaways is how potent other people's opinions can be. If I compare photos of me during that time with the way I look now, athlete-me looks emaciated. My current body is my favourite body, and it is much heavier than the body I was running from back then. At that time I was convinced I was overweight and that my body was wrong, all because I allowed external voices to affect what I saw in the mirror. It's taken many years of consistent practice and effort (and I still have to work on it), but loving myself out loud in the mirror every day has definitely helped me accept and be happy with my body.

I love you so much and I am proud of you will slowly replace the negative self-talk in your head and allow you to see that you are already enough.

BLOCKING OUT EXTERNAL voices is one thing; actually taking the time to put yourself first is quite another. What I'm about to say applies to everyone, but it especially applies to mothers. If I had to pick one category of people who have historically put themselves last, it's the mamas of the world. They keep the home and the family unit together and organized, they ensure the family is well-fed and clothed, and that everyone is where they are supposed to be when they are supposed to be, among so many other things. Moms do all this before they even consider their own needs. Some women have even given up their personal identity for the role of mom to the point that doing anything for themselves first is considered failure.

But sometimes we need to look out for our own interests. We need to set boundaries, establish "me time" and let those in our circle know that during that time all other concerns will take a back seat. Doing this will not only provide you with space and time to give your own life the attention it deserves, but, especially if you are a mother, it will give your children a better picture of the whole person you are. Reminding our little replicas that we are indeed people with hopes and dreams who also require attention and care is a very healthy thing to model.

While we are discussing the modelling of healthy behaviour, let's not forget the men. Many men were raised with the notion that they had to be a "stereotypical man" and were subsequently subjected to many toxic masculine traits that limit the expression of real emotion. Anger and a stoic demeanour? Fine. Giving ourselves permission to cry in public or in private, and expressing joy? Frowned upon. Telling our friends we love them and/or embracing them instead of just giving them the hard-pat? Scoffed at. We have been conditioned to shut off so many of our feelings. I encourage all men to explore all the emotions, all the "feels," that we've been robbing ourselves of.

The feelings we have suppressed to fit in or avoid social ripples need a place to go. Let's accept that they are there for a reason and deserve our attention. Let's give them a place to go.

I recommend we start with laughing out loud. Laugh so the neighbours can hear you. Smile from ear to ear and guffaw from the depths of your gut. So much of our world tells us to be small and quiet, and never disrupt the status quo, but sometimes you have to remove your filter and laugh until it hurts for no other reason than to reconnect with a true piece of yourself. While we're at it, let's open the floodgates to the rest of our emotions.

Another lesson we can learn from our younger selves is to acknowledge our feelings when they show up. I'm not suggesting we fall to the ground and have a temper tantrum when things don't go our way, but we can take a cue from how quickly our little ones feel something and then move through that negative experience and get right back to the thing they were doing before. We are more than enough—when things are great and, just as much, when things are in the tank. All we can do is to work through our emotions when they arrive in the healthiest way possible.

Sometimes you need to give yourself a pass to feel like crap. It's okay not to be okay. We often assume that we aren't allowed to be messy and that we always have to keep it together. The truth is you can be messy; you don't need to have it together and you don't have to pretend. Come as you are. Give yourself a break when you need one. If that means you show up and you're not your best self, then so be it. It's okay. Tomorrow is still a blank page and you get to write something new.

IIIII

GROUCHO MARX ONCE said "If you're not having fun, you're not doing it right." I agree. Regardless of the job, duty or responsibility, try to find a little joy in it. So many people are quick to tell stories about the fun they used to have. They used to be a "good time" before the kids. They used to play more before the new job. They used to find time in their day to let loose a little. So many excuses. The longer you tell yourself you are okay with this funless version of yourself, the more ingrained it will become.

Let me remind you that you are in control of what your present and future look like. Maybe nobody told you that you are allowed to have a good time while playing this video game called life. Not only can you have a good time, you can also make it easier for yourself during the process.

One of the best ways to ensure our lives are a little more fun is to reject the idea that we can't have fun. When we walk into a situation with the expectation that it won't be a good time, there is a high probability we will be right. What we tell ourselves is very powerful, and we believe what we tell ourselves hook, line and sinker.

EVEN WHEN YOU accept that you are more than enough, the rest of the world isn't always going to agree with you. Not everyone is going to understand you, what you are doing or why you are doing it—and that's fine. As long as you know your reasons and those reasons fit into the larger picture of the life you are creating for yourself, you are on the right track. Trying to ensure that everyone understands you is exhausting and fruitless. Love who you want to love, kiss who you want to kiss, dress how you want to dress, and listen to the music that feeds your soul. It is your life and yours alone, and those who don't understand it can kick rocks.

10

PRACTISE CURIOSITY

I have vivid memories of watching Saturday-morning cartoons, happily sitting in front of the TV with a snack and anxiously awaiting the start of *Astro Boy, The Jetsons, Babar* or *Curious George. Curious George* always resonated with me. A cartoon about an orphaned monkey that would always find himself in a little bit of trouble because he couldn't resist trying to discover new and exciting things. The Man in the Yellow Hat would always be there to warn George about the dangers of the world, but that monkey, ever curious, continued to explore whatever was in front of him.

Our curiosity seems to dwindle as we age, which is unfortunate because curiosity is what pushes us beyond our limiting beliefs and drives us to new experiences. *What if?* is a powerful motivator. Curiosity is the gateway to resourcefulness. It helps us find creative solutions to overcome the challenges in our lives.

Curiosity served me well when I was running one of my fitness companies, P.H.A.T. Training. As any business owner knows, you are always trying to find ways to attract new clients. I was a new father of two back then, and finding time to incorporate parenting, fitness and running a studio was becoming increasingly difficult. Then I had an idea to meld them together. In the past, I'd seen fitness camps for mothers and their children, but rarely had I seen anything centred on fathers. I was curious whether there were good reasons for this or if I'd discovered a hole in the market, so I created our first Daddy and Me boot camp in the summer of 2014. The camp wasn't well attended, but we did get featured in a news segment that ended up giving my business a boost years later.

In the spring of 2018 I got a call from a California area code. It was Lionsgate Studios. The producer said that Kevin Hart and Hart Productions were creating a TV show called *What the Fit,* and they had stumbled upon a video clip of my Daddy and Me boot camp and wanted to know if I'd be interested in flying down to Hollywood to run a similar camp with Kevin Hart, DJ Khaled and a bunch of toddlers. I said *yes.* A few weeks later I flew to Hart's studio to shoot the content and make some new connections. That episode of *What the Fit*—which wouldn't have included me had Kevin Hart and his producers not seen my video, which had 31 views at the time—currently has 8 million views online. I like to mention that to people who think that you need to have millions of followers or views for your content to matter. I still use that episode to help leverage many other aspects in my life.

Many content creators are more concerned with what they think other people want to see than with what they really want to create. If they post something that doesn't go viral, they consider it a failure and try something else. I firmly believe that you should make what matters to you. You should make the things you are curious about and the things that excite you. You may not have millions of people paying attention, but you will find your audience. You will find the people who really relate to what you are making, and then you can build from there.

A little curiosity turned into a large marketing campaign for my fitness studio and father-specific boot camp. A campaign that a Canadian small-business owner could never have afforded. I don't know what Kevin Hart and DJ Khaled's going rate for a ten-minute commercial is, but I can imagine it's likely out of my price range.

CURIOSITY IS LIKE a loose thread in a sweater. Once you pull it, it just keeps giving.

In 2017 I was shooting a small promo called Plaid for Dad in support of Prostate Cancer Canada with a former NHL star,

Jason Strudwick. At the time he was the host of *Dinner Televi-sion,* which aired six days a week on a cable network. After we finished shooting the segment, he told me that he'd just quit the show and was moving on to radio. I'd always watched those kinds of shows and thought, *Hey, I could do that.* However, the opportunity had never presented itself and I wasn't sure how to pursue that type of position. Turns out that sometimes igno-rance *is* bliss and, in some cases, just the thing you need in order to make an audacious step.

When Jason dropped the information that he'd left his chair as co-host and they were still looking for someone to fill it, I saw my in. To say I was curious is an understatement. A wave of excitement, fear and possibility overcame me. I asked Jason who I would need to speak with in order to take his old job. He told me I should ask for the boss, Stan Papulkas.

As soon as we wrapped shooting, I drove straight to Citytv Edmonton (where the show was filmed), walked in the door and asked the receptionist if I could speak with Stan. She asked me if I had an appointment. When I told her I did not, she told me that Stan was very busy. I replied that I didn't mind waiting until he had a moment.

The great thing about going in without any expectations is that I hadn't set myself up for disappointment. I was on a mis-sion purely fuelled by curiosity. I wanted to see how far I could take this idea. Every moment, every piece of new information I got, was a bonus. Each step I took was a new opportunity to learn. I was in an office I would never have otherwise entered, and I was about to meet a man who was connected to a field of work I was interested in. As far as I could see, this could only be a win–win.

After a while, Stan came out. I told him, straight-up, "I want to take Jason's job and they can stop the search for a new host." He asked me if I had ever hosted this type of show before. I said I hadn't, but I was confident that I could figure it out. At this stage they were "stunt-casting" local celebrities until they found the right fit. He mentioned that my name had come up as a possible co-host when they were brainstorming. I liked the idea of trying out the job, but I didn't like the idea of doing it for free. If I was going to try it, I wanted to be all-in and I wanted them to be as well. I proposed a deal to Stan: I would work the next three shows for free and, if they liked what they saw, they'd cancel the search for a new host and pay me for the job. He agreed. After the first show I was signed on as the new host of *Dinner Television*. I learned a lot about live, on-air hosting from my more experienced co-hosts and got an opportunity to dabble in a career that I had always been curious about. Even though the show ended up not being renewed, I felt lucky to have wedged myself in before the chapter closed on that particular media delivery.

WE HAVE ALL left a meeting, job interview or audition and wondered what would have happened if we'd done this or said that. *What if?* always floats through the air. Oftentimes, speculation and assumptions are all we get for an answer. I decided to lean into answering that question in my professional life. Instead of wondering *what if?*, I started saying whatever my gut told me to say. I started to behave authentically instead of letting my emotions create barriers and inhibitions.

The first time I remember making a conscious decision to act on *what if?* in the moment and receiving a positive outcome was during a film audition many years back. It was for a feature film called *Resurrecting the Champ*, starring Samuel L. Jackson and Josh Hartnett, that was filming in Calgary, Alberta (about a three-hour drive from my hometown). Typically, big U.S. productions come up to Canada to take advantage of our beautiful landscapes and tax incentives. The downside is that the majority of the cast has already been chosen and the local actors get to fight for the scraps.

I don't recall the role I was auditioning for, but it was another easily forgettable character with one or two lines. I do remember that I didn't want to do it. I was grateful for the opportunity, but this kind of gig wasn't why I got into the business nor would it be the kind of work I would be proud to show my children when they grew up. I was really getting down on myself, and then they called my name and invited me into the room to read. I greeted and thanked them for the opportunity to audition. Then, unexpectedly, something came over me. In that moment I had to be honest with them and myself. I informed them that, although I appreciated the chance, this wasn't the type of role I wanted. I explained that I'd been working on my craft for many years and found I was being offered one-line roles of little consequence that didn't reflect what I knew I could do. I thanked them again and declined the audition. They were taken aback but respected my choice. We shook hands and I was on my way. I got back into my car and phoned my agent to tell her what had happened. She was not happy. She couldn't believe I'd done that (which is fair, as it's not typical behaviour in the industry), and after a few sharp words we ended the call. I started driving back to Edmonton. Fifteen minutes later, my agent called me back. I was expecting to get another earful. Instead, she informed me that I needed to turn around. Casting wanted to see me about another role.

When I got back to the audition space, I was handed script pages for a much bigger role in the film. I took a few minutes to get familiar with the new role before heading back into the room. After I read my lines, production staff thanked me and told me not to drive back to Edmonton just yet, as they might want to see me again. The rest of the hopefuls went in and delivered their auditions. Then my agent let me know that production had made their top picks and wanted me to come back tomorrow to compete head-to-head for the bigger and more substantial role. When it was all said and done, I got the role. And I learned that together curiosity and agency can create the changes in your life that you deserve, if you have the guts to go for it.

One of my most special *what if?* moments occurred while I was filming *Black Summer*, Season Two, for Netflix. I was a huge fan of the first season, and I'd even auditioned for the lead role, unsuccessfully. When an audition for another character for Season Two was announced, I jumped at the opportunity.

When the script hit my inbox, I found out I was reading for the part of "Huge Guy." Normally I don't get excited when I see character names like this. Afterall, how integral of a character could Huge Guy be? But due to my appreciation of the show, I went ahead with the audition. A few days later, I got the call that I'd booked the role. John, our director, set up a video call with the new cast to discuss the show and his approach. One of the first things he mentioned was that all of the characters were named vaguely on purpose. He didn't know who would be chosen and didn't want to put too much on the characters until they were fully cast. Two of the final episodes had yet to be written, and he mentioned there might be a chance for one of our roles to grow into something larger. One character from the previous season, Sun, wasn't supposed to survive. However, Christine Lee, the actor who played the part, had done such an amazing job that they were compelled to write her in more. She was a fan favourite.

Once John dropped that cherry of possibility, it shaped my every move going forward. John also allowed us to create our own backstory and character name, which was something I'd never had the privilege of doing with a streaming-service film. It just so happened that I had already visualized a moment like this. I knew that one day I would be able to offer up a character name to which I had a special connection. I knew that, if given the chance, I would bring Mance to life. Or, more accurately, reintroduce Mance to the world in an entirely different light.

As a Black man in Canada who doesn't have a clear idea of where his family came from, I've spent a fair bit of time researching my family tree and other people who share my last name. In doing so, I stumbled upon a blues singer named Mance Lipscombe and dug a little deeper into who he was. His music was mesmerizing and his story—the little I could find—was captivating. I was reminded of a Hemingway quote someone once told me: "Every person has two deaths, when he is buried in the ground and the last time someone says his name." After hearing that quote, I knew that I wanted to create a character named Mance in an attempt to keep Mance Lipscombe's memory alive and to tie a bit of who I am to who he was.

The real Mance Lipscombe was born Beau De Glen Lipscomb. (Some of the Lipscombes I researched added an "e" at the end and some didn't—variations in spellings are typical in ancestry searches.) As a youth he took the name Mance (short for "emancipation"). I knew that this show, *Black Summer,* was the perfect opportunity to bring Mance to the world.

I came to the first day of principal photography with a weighted backstory of survival and truth. My character would attempt to survive a massive zombie apocalypse. In the original script, he was supposed to die somewhere in the middle of Season Two, but I could always hear John in my head saying "If we create a character that needs to survive, they will." The first day on set we shot a massive battle scene. I remember looking around at all the people of colour being shot or dying. Right after the cameras were cut, I said as loud as I could, "We can't kill Mance. We've got to keep the Black in Black Summer!" The producers laughed, and I used it as my opportunity to get to know each and every one of them.

Whenever I am on any set, I make it my mission to meet everyone, learn their names and spend a bit of positive time with them. As Maya Angelou said, "People will forget what you said, people will forget what you did, but people will never forget how you made them feel." Something I have also learned on set is that, at least at my level, you need to do more than the job you were contracted for. Networking, positive interpersonal interactions and self-promotion can all aid your career trajectory. Typically after booking a role, people go into "actor mode" and focus on the task at hand. There's absolutely no fault in doing this, and many people advise actors to take that approach. Me, however? I know there is more available. I know that the current job can lead to new jobs, and movie-making is a "who you know" kind of business. I make a habit of knowing and making an impact on as many people as I can, in addition to doing the job I'm paid to do.

While having a chat with one of the producers, I mentioned that I was a former professional athlete. They were intrigued about how high I could jump. Later, when we were setting up for a shot where Mance was required to climb under a barbed-wire fence before making his way to a safe spot, without being spotted by zombies or hostiles, I suggested something different: "What if I just jump over the fence?" "You can do that?" they asked. In my head, I scoffed. The fence was nipple-high at best.

Easy-peasy, even at my advanced age. I proceeded to do it. They loved the shot and used it.

I later learned that was the moment when they decided to scrap the idea of killing Mance. Not only did they decide to keep Mance around, but they had the opportunity to write a scene they'd been dreaming of: an epic battle-royale chase.

Spoiler alert: This might be the sickest zombie-fight scene in the history of movies and television combined. It took three days to film what became eleven minutes of jaw-clenching awesomeness. Mance survives to (hopefully) become one of the lead storylines if and when a third season of *Black Summer* ever happens.

Asking *what if?* enabled me to be a part of, and survive, one of the best zombie shows ever created. An innovative show that Stephen King praised and said "showrunners could learn a lot from."

OCCASIONALLY, AMID OUR discussions about monsters, the universe and video games, my youngest son, Indiana, surprises us with thought-provoking gems. Recently, he asked a question that sparked introspection: "What is your favourite moment in your life?" He recounted the joy of meeting his best friend, M. Meanwhile, my eldest son, Chile, cited the unforgettable summer at camp where he spent two weeks with a new group of friends. Tripp, my middle son, said his tenth birthday was his favourite memory. When my turn came, I responded with the "correct" answer, something about the day each of them was born, *blah blah blah*. Then, a memory that felt true to my core hit me. I told them the story of when I was solo-travelling to Bilbao, Spain, for a track meet. I recounted driving into a city that felt like it was carved out of the mountains that surrounded it. I told them about all the amazing colours, the huge dogs made out of flowers and the jaw-dropping architecture. Lying in my bed, eyes open, I debated whether to explore or get to sleep so I would be fully rested for the next day's event. Outside my window, I could hear smatterings of people walking down the street. FOMO got the best of me. I opted to leave my bed, get dressed and see what the commotion was about. I walked out of my lodging and joined a group of five or six Spanish folk. They motioned for me to follow them. I obliged, and we walked, skipped and yelled our way to the subway station. With each stop, the train seemed to fill with more and more people on the same journey.

I had no idea where I was, where I was going or how I was going to get back. I just continued to follow my curiosity. An hour or so later, we encountered the swelling sound of celebrations. In the clearing ahead, I saw a huge sandy beach with ten-foot-tall bonfires spaced twenty feet apart. The air was filled with the sounds of cheering, fireworks and drum circles, several of which I joined.

By chance, the day I arrived in Bilbao was the Night of San Juan. A day to celebrate the summer solstice. A day of tradition and good times. Through basic attempts at communicating, I was able to discern that we were to jump over or through the fire to rid ourselves of the negative from the previous year, and then to dip our feet in the water to purify ourselves and prepare for the year ahead. By the end of the night, I had forgotten about any language barrier. I was dancing and communicating with strangers, connected by a beautiful spectacle.

I knew absolutely nothing about the Night of San Juan, the people or what I was getting into, but letting my curiosity lead gifted me with the experience of a lifetime.

How did I do in the track meet? I don't remember—and that's the point. If I had been too focused on performing at the meet, I would have missed the real journey. Of course, solid focus on my professional track-and-field career could have taken me further, but at what cost? I can't remember who won that event. I can't name the top three high jumpers in the world that year, or any given year. But I can remember the experiences that the sport gave me as I travelled the world and witnessed a multitude of different cultures. The unexpected turns I've taken, thanks to following my curiosity, are some of my most cherished memories.

There was a common thread in my family's best memories that I find interesting: each of our stories was based on connections and celebrations with other people, and all without the use of technology. You won't find your next special moment with your head buried in your phone. You'll find it out there, in the world, by doing and connecting with other curious humans.

||||||

DO NOT BE afraid to ask *what if?* Whether you are working, or deciding whether to take that trip, or thinking about asking that special person on a date—regardless of what you are wondering—acting on your curiosity has the potential to effect positive change in your life. By asking *what if?* you make yourself available for all the possibilities you can dream up.

PART 3
PRODUCTIVITY

Is the glass half-empty or half-full?

I always struggle with this question because it feels like a trap. The two choices limit me to a reality I don't buy into. For me, the glass is always full. It's half-full of one thing and half-full of all the other things present in that moment. The question should be more specific. I understand the idea is to determine if you are a negative or positive thinker. Do you see possibility and abundance or do you focus on scarcity and negative outcomes?

The glass is always full. There is always something you can gain, learn and use to make tomorrow a little better than today.

11

OBLITERATE OBSTACLES

*"I always believed that when you follow your heart
or your gut, when you really follow the things that feel
great to you, you can never lose, because settling
is the worst feeling in the world."*

—RIHANNA

O nce momentum has us rolling in the right direction, it may feel like nothing can stop us. One thing, however, is certain: no matter how smooth the road is, you can bet an obstacle is around the corner. It's never a question of *if* one is coming but rather *when* and *how* you will deal with it when it does. Whether we are talking about personal goals, business goals or relationship goals, obstacles and roadblocks are sure to happen. The quicker we accept that challenges are a natural part of any endeavour, the easier it will be to deal with them when they arrive and the faster we can move through them.

In this chapter I am sharing some of the wise words the people who have influenced my life have shared with me. I hope they will positively affect your life as they did mine.

WILLIE H. HILL has been coaching at Morehouse College in Atlanta, Georgia, since 1979. He spent eleven seasons with the football team before switching to the track program in 1989. He is known as Will "The Thrill" Hill for his exploits as an NAIA All-American running back and nationally ranked sprinter at Central State University in Ohio. After a brief stint with the NFL's Cincinnati Bengals in the early seventies, Hill returned to his alma mater in 1974 and began his coaching career.

Hill is more than a coach. Over the years many players and students alike have considered him a father figure and mentor. In fact, he's so well-known at Morehouse that every athlete and most students who have matriculated through its red-brick quarters could, without fail, give you their impersonation of the unique manner in which this mountain of a man speaks. In an oxymoronish high-pitched voice, and making use of copious rhetorical questions, Hill will share nuggets of Southern wisdom and talk about motivation, success and overcoming obstacles.

Okay, baby. If I got in a fight with God, I might not win but he would what? He would know that I was there . . .

I remember coach laying down these words of wisdom as we sat on the hot mondo track during practice. He was getting us ready for the approaching battle. At the time I thought he was talking about our upcoming competition. Looking back, I realize he was preparing us for the battle of life. He was making it clear that even when it looks like everything is stacked against you, it's still your duty to give it your all. He challenged my idea of what *winning* meant. His words highlighted the importance of leaving your mark and making an impact that will be remembered. The more I think about what he said, the more I understand how important it is to leave a lasting impression. I am reminded to bring my all into every interaction, even when I feel like the deck has been stacked against me.

Ahhh, baby, what? If you ain't hurtin', then you ain't workin'.

Coach reminded us that nobody wants to hear excuses, especially from a Black man. He wanted us to stay humble, to make sure we did the work and that the work didn't do us.

Whether it's reality TV or social media, so much of what we watch doles out the fantasy of overnight success. We've been conditioned to believe that we should jump ship when things aren't as easy as we hoped they'd be. Coach Hill reminded us that it was never supposed to be easy and that anyone who tried selling you that lie was delusional. He kept us all grounded and focused on being prepared to do more than was expected.

A Morehouse motto is *To be early is to be on time, to be on time is to be late and to be late is unacceptable.* Does this mean that everything started on time at Morehouse? Hell to the nah. But it did remind us, Black men specifically, that we would have to do more and pull more than our share in order to achieve the things we wanted in the current social climate.

When asked why we had to run up a hill carrying one of our teammates on our back, and what that had to do with track and field, Coach Hill responded:

Baby, 'cause what? Now you know how it's going to feel when that gorilla jump on yo' back when you hit that last 100 metres [of the 400-metre dash]. See, when that fool pull up beside you, you can take him somewhere he's never been.

Coach was trying to instill the importance of preparation. You can't expect to perform in adverse situations if you've never been tested in adverse situations. I remember the day we were doing those drills. I was trying to sprint up the hill with one of the biggest shot putters or discus throwers draped over my back. With every attempt up the hill, my legs ached, my lungs burned and I wanted to quit. Shortly after that, the skies opened up and the rain began to pour down. Normally in weather like this, technical practice would be cancelled. As a high jumper, the take-off apron is a delicate place and the chance of slipping can be high. I thought Coach was wild for forcing us to practice in that horrific weather. I was grumpy and didn't have the best attitude during those sessions. It wasn't until the NCAA championships that I experienced the short-term gains of his words and techniques.

That high-jump competition began just as a heavy downpour started pummelling the track. The other athletes were scrambling to keep their stuff dry. They were complaining and adjusting their run-ups to prepare for the challenging conditions. I remember walking over to Coach and him giving me a knowing look before reassuring me that I was more prepared than any of the other athletes. We had already trained in this; we had already succeeded in this. For us, this was just another day on the track. And coach was right: I won my first NCAA national championship that day!

Coach Hill taught me how much I could carry. Although similar to the old standby "what doesn't kill you makes you stronger," his version, slathered with Southern charm, hit differently.

I HAD THE privilege of working with and getting to know legendary diversity leader and educator Jane Elliott. During one of our conversations she shared something that still resonates with me today. She asked me if I knew the golden rule. I responded the way many of you would. I said, "Yeah, treat other people the way you would like to be treated." Jane corrected me. She said, "Treat other people the way *they* would like to be treated."

It's such a simple adjustment, but it makes so much more sense. This small reframe can help you overcome the many obstacles you will face when trying to do "the right thing."

We may have the best intentions when we attempt to influence positive change, but sometimes our actions fall short. This usually happens because our intentions stem from a very personal place. When the impact of our actions doesn't match our original intent, we start getting defensive and then real obstacles arise in our attempt to help. We end up treating other people the way we would want to be treated in a similar scenario. On paper, this doesn't seem so bad, but in practice people experience the world through many different vantage points. *Treating people the way they wish to be treated* allows us to decentre and focus on the person we were trying to positively impact.

Too often we walk through life making choices assuming that other people would like their lives to be laid out exactly the way we do. We do this often without consulting the folks we are trying to help. Changing our focus to what others want urges us to dig a little deeper. It asks us to connect with individuals and discover what they need before making decisions. Swapping the word "you" with "they" stops us from assuming that everyone else sees the world the same way we do.

I was reminded of Jane's wise words when my wife and I were organizing a major anti-discrimination conference in 2018 called The #MakeItAwkward Inclusivity Summit. Given the social climate of the time and the platform that I had, we wanted to do something meaningful and impactful. With the help of a small core group, we organized a summit for corporate leaders, students and many others. We invited experts in anti-discrimination to share their knowledge at the conference. I had never organized an event of this scale before, but I had a vision of what I wanted and started moving in that direction. We invited Jane to be a featured guest speaker as well as actors, comedians and musicians such as Quinton Aaron, Stannis Smith, Rell Battle and Sterling Scott, to name a few.

The summit was a big undertaking, and we had to deal with a number of unforeseen obstacles, including in my own family, in order to get it off the ground.

It was 2:40 a.m. on a frosty January morning in Edmonton, Alberta. Our youngest son, Indiana, had been screaming in agony for hours, and we had just arrived at Stollery Children's Hospital. The day before I had taken him to the nearest medi-centre to be checked out. His daycare providers said that Indiana's lip was bleeding and he was developing sores on his legs and arms. Although I am not a doctor, a couple of my friends are, so I feel like I have surface-level knowledge of a considerable number of ailments. I've been known to confidently diagnose my friends and family with the help of a friend-text and a Google search. My latest text-message exchange and online research seemed to contradict the medi-centre physician's diagnosis of Indy.

The doctor's verdict? Slap cheek syndrome, a condition that looks like someone slapped your face and left a red mark, and does not require medical treatment. With that diagnosis, Indy and I went home and gritted out the rest of the day until his mother, Julia, got back from work. As the day went on, Indy looked and felt worse. He could not sleep, and his ear-piercing screams cut through our bones as if we were sleep-training an infant all over again, but these screams seemed worse. While this was happening we were still in the process of organizing the conference. Our concern for Indy and the stress over event details were mounting.

If you have never organized an event of this size, you might be surprised by the $200,000 price tag required to pull it off. I surely was. However, our goal was to provide the city and beyond with a memorable and educational event, and we knew how many tickets we had to sell in order to break even. The pressure of putting on an event of this size, especially when you are green to the process, was heavy. Juggling that while worrying about the well-being of our youngest child took it to another level. The cherry on top was the social media gorilla that suddenly leaped onto our back. As we were getting ready to go to the hospital, I saw a Twitter message that read *It doesn't matter if you stream an event. When you boast inclusivity for your event you need to make ticket prices affordable so those interested in attending IN PERSON can be present. #makeitawkward*

We found ourselves mired in the fallout of that one misinformed tweet derailing us and our project. That tweet, which came to us while we were caring for our little man in the hospital, caught on like wildfire. People started sharing, retweeting and making up stories that I was in cahoots with our mayor, embezzling funds from taxpayers (the city had purchased a large number of tickets for students) and attempting to get famous off racism. Rumours started circulating that I had staged the verbal hate-attack on me, the one that birthed the entire #MakeItAwkward movement, for social clout. Let me tell you, if I knew how to create viral videos at will, videos that can capture the attention of the country and beyond, you would already know my name. Also, who in their right mind would want to play the villain in such a staged event? All of that is moot, however. Once these online accusations caught fire, people began boycotting and trying to cancel our event. News outlets, our sponsors and our invited guests were receiving calls from people trying to persuade them to rethink their involvement. Our ticket sales halted, and we scrambled to restore the integrity of the event and salvage what we could so it could take place.

I felt like I was being attacked from multiple angles. The combined chatter on social media and in the press made me feel like I was backed into a corner. Everything in me wanted to lash out and snap back at every person spreading nonsense online. I wanted the news outlets covering their baseless claims to be remanded. Then I remembered Jane's restructuring of the golden rule—"Treat other people the way *they* want to be treated"—and it all began to settle in my mind. Most people are the heroes in their own story, and they believe they are acting from a just and fair place. The people talking about me and the movement didn't know me; all they knew was what they were feeling. There is no time in my life when I felt angry, sad or confused that I didn't want love and care in return. I opted to take the loving road. When I wanted to shut out folks, I listened to their concerns and tried to find the truth behind the feelings. We pressed on with the event, knowing that the noisy few did not represent the quiet many. People were looking forward to what we were about to create and we would not let them down. Being patient and listening to the concerns of many folks ended up helping the event and taught me lessons about dealing with similar obstacles in the future. When all was said and done, the event went well and Indy came away just fine!

SOMETIMES LIFE HANDS us major opportunities—some people call them *problems* or *obstacles*. Whatever you call them, when they show up, we often steer away from the things that bring us joy. Maybe we stopped painting because life got heavy. Maybe we have writer's block due to stressors in our lives. Whatever the reason, we tend to wait until the dark clouds pass before we get back into doing the things we love. I suggest we do the exact opposite: Lean into the darkness. Reframe those problems and obstacles as opportunities. Make it a habit to look at life through those lenses.

Some people want to wait for inspiration before they start something. They want to wait until they feel motivated or see a spark. Other people do not wait to begin. They do things when they are happy, they do things when they are sad, they do things when they are mad. They do things when they are stressed out, when they feel unmotivated, when they are tired—they do not let their current mood influence their dedication to act.

I think songwriters do it the best. Both Beyoncé and Adele have made a living writing about heartache and pain. Most of the country music genre is littered with regret and loss. The Blues expressed the struggles of the time, and rap music offered a vehicle for narrating the hardships of a singer's life. We celebrate and enjoy the fruits of that labour, the labour of leaning into the darkness.

When I think of some of the hardest times of my life, I know that it's highly unlikely that I'll ever be in that exact emotional state again. Those moments were rare, and so are the feelings I was steeped in at the time. I like to ask myself, *How can you use those feelings to create something you can be proud of, something that will resonate with everyone who experiences it?* When you find yourself running away or avoiding the things you love in the presence of pain, shift and do the opposite. Let painful moments become a beacon of creation. If you perceive greatness in your creations, remind yourself that few people celebrate the achievements of average folks. No one writes about the mundane; no one reveres art that doesn't evoke real emotion. When you are in an irregular, emotionally charged, dark place, use it, lean into it, and be courageous enough to keep creating through it. Not only will you be proud of what you made, but you'll find the entire process very therapeutic.

||||||

PLANS RARELY GO exactly as we map them out. There are often setbacks and unforeseen hurdles to overcome. Obliterating your obstacles starts with not allowing them to be the focus of your journey. The best hockey players know you need to pass the puck to where the player is going to be, not where they are. The same goes for shooting your shot at your dreams. You have to look where you are going, not at the obstacle standing in your way.

If you look hard enough, you will see there are obstacles everywhere. If you are in a room right now, you are surrounded by four walls and a door. Leaving the room might seem insurmountable if you don't have the right knowledge and a little motivation. You can't walk through walls, but you know you can make your way to the door, open it and proceed to your next obstacle. Yes, this is a simple example, but only because most of us have the tools to leave our room. We've done it so many times, we don't even think twice about it. It's only when new challenges come up that we panic. Panic no more. Practice using some of the tools covered in the following chapters and treat the next obstacle like the opportunity it is.

12

YOU HAVE ENOUGH TIME

"What I know for sure is that speaking your truth
is the most powerful tool we all have."
—OPRAH WINFREY

I've heard people say that the best invention in the world would be the twenty-fifth hour. If we could create more time, we could solve so many problems. In fact, people say the biggest reason why they don't create something, start a new project or entertain that new business is that they feel they don't have enough time. With work, kids, elderly parents, pets or social commitments, they simply don't have enough hours in a day to begin something new. I disagree. Time isn't the real issue here—it's emotional bandwidth. When something feels overwhelming, the idea of starting it can feel suffocating. Even if you could tack on a few more hours to every day, it wouldn't lessen the feeling that it's all too much. You'd just have more time to feel it.

Think of the busiest, most productive humans you can. Once you've identified them remember that they too only have twenty-four hours in their day. The difference between you and these people is the way they choose to use their hours. Luckily, there are some simple strategies you can incorporate into your busy life that will help you maximize your time and lower the emotional pressure that seems to be the real culprit of inaction.

Here is a collection of my favourite methods to increase emotional bandwidth, which may leave you feeling like you just invented that twenty-fifth hour.

Big Littles

When we have big dreams, we can get stuck by the size of the undertaking. As a teacher and speaker on diversity, equity and inclusion, I understand what it's like to contemplate a task that seems impossible to complete. Sometimes, I wonder if my actions are even making a dent in the problem. Other times, I get discouraged about where I'm at in the entertainment world. I compare it to where I want to be, and the distance between the two seems insurmountable. Even though these thoughts enter my mind, I don't let them stay there. I acknowledge them and understand that it's just negative self-talk trying to sabotage my progress. Instead, I try to break down large tasks into bite-size chunks that allow me a bit more freedom and give me a sense of accomplishment as I strike things off the list. I call this "Big Littles."

Big Littles is simply taking the macro and breaking it into micros. The macro could be writing a book, taking a trip, learning a new language or starting a new business. Whatever the project, you need to start by focusing on a date. It can be any date that means something to you; just pick one. Once you have a finish line, you have something to aim for. The next step is to write down all the tasks that need to be done in order to complete the project. This is when you let out all the things that could go wrong. Identify them, write them down, and then plan how to deal with them. But don't just plan; try to anticipate when the problems will happen. Capture everything on a spreadsheet , create a schedule and put it in a calendar.

Work through and break down everything until each item becomes something you can tackle with the least amount of emotional weight and energy. Once you've created a visual plan, you can rest easy knowing that the time you have allotted to the "littles" will work toward the completion of the "big." This strategy should result in a more digestible plan for your daily activities that will ultimately stack up in the completion of your "shoot for the stars" idea.

Once you have everything scheduled in your calendar, you have to treat the action points seriously. You can't miss an appointment with yourself. You have to treat yourself with the same level of respect you would your boss. Too often we let these appointments with ourselves take a back seat to everything else in our life. We fail to make ourselves the

THE ART OF DOING

priority, and all of our dreams get pushed aside without a second thought.

Breaking down your big goal into smaller action points and scheduling those points into your calendar will ultimately allow you to spend more time on the things you want without taxing your emotional bandwidth. Then you won't have to spend your free time stressing over all the things you could and should be doing. You'll be able to enjoy your time off knowing you are doing all you need to do to bring your idea across the finish line.

A word to the wise: Avoid using words like *someday* or *one day*. Neither of those days are on the calendar. *Tomorrow* is very elusive, too. Every time you wake up, tomorrow finds a way to jump just out of reach but stays close enough to make you think you'll be able to hit the gas. Make an actual appointment with yourself. You have to respect your process more than anyone else's if you want to create real and lasting change in your life. The next easiest step shouldn't be too far in the future either. Make it, and yourself, a priority and then move it forward.

Do What You Suck At

We love to do what we excel at. It obviously doesn't feel good to shoot 120 or more on a golf course. I love golf because it humbles even the best athletes. It's one of those sports that, regardless of your athletic ability, you will not be good at when you try it for the first time. That may be an understatement. If you decide to play golf and you have never swung a club before, there is a 100 percent chance that you will suck at it. You have to want to be good and you have to be okay knowing you won't be. You can bet on being inconsistent and confused for a very long time. If you dedicate time to working on the areas where you lag, you may end up being not bad. You won't see instant results, and it will take many years to reap the benefits, regardless of how much you spend on gear. Ah, golf. It's a love affair that makes little sense, but here's the deal: People adore golf because it's a quirky blend of frustration and euphoria.

Golf seduces you with its lush green landscapes, fancy clubs, and promises of becoming a pro. Sure, a few people actually become good, even great, but I tend not to focus on the outliers. If you want to find something to suck at, golf is a solid choice. It's like a never-ending quest to conquer the impossible. Each swing becomes an epic saga with a plot twist no one saw coming. You hit the ball, it disappears into the abyss of tall grass, and you find yourself playing hide-and-seek like a sad puppy looking for its bone.

But, hey, the few glorious moments when that tiny ball somehow finds its way to the hole are like fireworks exploding in your soul. It's like hitting the jackpot at a casino you didn't even know you were in. You forget all the mis-hits, all the balls lost in the water, and you think, *Hey, maybe I could go pro.* I am humbled to say that I held that thought at one point while playing this beautiful game.

I was just starting to figure out my driver, and I was hitting 30 to 40 percent of the balls straight-ish. To be fair, I was launching some bombs out there, consistently, between 310 to 340 yards. A friend of mine suggested that I should enter some of the long-drive competitions (competitions that consist of only driving the ball). Typically, in those competitions you have a longer, stiffer and more flat-degreed driver, and you crush the ball as far as you can. This felt like my next logical move. I Googled where to train for this and found a golf shop with a pro that offered lessons in long-driving. I went to my first scheduled appointment confident, excited, and ready to show the world how I could whack the ball. I pulled out one of the two drivers I'd brought with me. My instructor poured out some balls and asked me to show him what I could do. My confidence started to decline a bit as I stood on the turfed tee box with a professional awaiting visual confirmation of what I had told him I could do. I addressed the ball and started my pre-swing routine, preparing to smash some balls right through the virtual golf screen. With the first ball on the tee, I wound up and smacked the life out of the . . . floor. My driver snapped in two and I was left standing there shocked and fully embarrassed. This was obviously a one-in-a-million fluke and, luckily, I had another driver with me. I loaded some balls up again and duffed them a few times before I felt like I had shaken my embarrassment. It was time to show the instructor what I had come here to do. I addressed the ball again, took a deep breath and unleashed another monster of a swing. I smashed the exact spot on the ground again and obliterated my second driver. The instructor looked at me with pity and, without being asked, told me that I would not be able to use one of their drivers. He offered to coach me on another technique, suggesting we use the remaining fifty minutes of our session working on my seven iron. The moral of the story: Golf is a game of ups and downs. You may think you are on top of the world but you will find out, rather quickly, that you are not.

I wanted to learn the game of golf, and I acknowledged how difficult it is. There were times when I wanted to quit, but instead I kept moving. After each step forward, I took a few steps backward. I am not a good golfer, but I am way better than I was. I can see the benefits of working on the things I sucked at because it allowed me to enjoy the entire game a little more each time. I can still drive the ball pretty far—whether it is straight or not is another story. However, the best club in my bag is definitely my seven iron. Funny what a little focused coaching from a professional can do for your game. (In 1999, some of the Morehouse track-and-field team and I worked the Masters Championship in Augusta, Georgia. I remember watching Tiger Woods strike the ball with such precision and ease as he navigated the course. I blame him for making me believe that I, too, could do it.)

That same logic can be applied to all aspects of life. Focusing our energies on the areas where we are underperforming will make our entire life journey more enjoyable and efficient.

When I was studying psychology in school, we did the Herrmann Brain Dominance Instrument assessment. The test identifies the subject's thinking style so they can understand how to modify their behaviour to achieve greater success. It's organized into four quadrants: analytical, sequential, interpersonal and imaginative. My imaginative and interpersonal skills were off the charts. Being adventurous, intuitive, and a good team player, and being in touch with my feelings seemed hardwired in my brain. However, the analytical and sequential side of my brain was as empty as a drum. Skills such as organizing, planning, using spreadsheets, inputting data, or taking time to make decisions were non-existent. It couldn't have been clearer which area of my brain was leading the charge. It was so lopsided that it looked like the printer ran out of ink when it printed the left side of the sheet. I made a conscious decision to focus on that blank part of the paper. I began to focus on what I sucked at. I tried to work on as many analytical and sequential activities as I could, making a real effort to focus on my weak points. The process wasn't fast, but it was steady. Bit by bit, the things that I used to shy away from because they didn't come naturally became more comfortable and a part of my life. If I had told college me that I would become an author, use spreadsheets, make plans, create budgets, and help other people organize their lives, he would have laughed in my face. Working on what I sucked at rather than playing solely in the areas where I excelled has had a major effect on my ability to achieve my goals.

Create a Better Version of Yourself

Summit at Sea is a multidisciplinary experience designed to foster deep connections with amazing like-minded people. It was one of the most eye- and mind-opening experiences of my life. It felt like I was privy to a secret club of movers and shakers. The organizers did a great job of creating an exclusive, invite-only vibe that only served to increase the allure of the event. I had to be invited by a current member and then vetted by one of the Summit staff before being accepted into the fold. Once I got the green light, I flew to Miami for an epic two-day cruise. This wasn't just any cruise, however. The folks aboard this boat had all done some amazing things. People who have spoken at the summit include Bill Clinton, Tim Ferriss, Richard Branson, Shonda Rhimes, Al Gore, Jeff Bezos, John Legend, Tarana Burke, Quincy Jones and Gary Vaynerchuk. Our house band was The Roots, and Pitbull and Imogen Heap also performed for the members onboard. I remember having lunch with a number of other entrepreneurs, all of whom were discussing their companies. The man to my left introduced himself and his company by saying "I made the browser. You know the thing you type www into? That's mine." Yeah, this was a boat filled with doers at the highest level, and I was eating it up.

I was able to attend this exclusive cruise because I wasn't afraid to ask for help to get on the cruise. In this instance, the help came from my friend Carissa Reiniger (CEO of Silver Lining, a company that helps small businesses grow). We had met many years ago when we were selected as "Top 20 under 30" people in Edmonton by *SEE Magazine*. I was impressed with her ability to organize and keep many lofty projects afloat. She wasn't shy about pinpointing areas in my game that needed upgrades, and I was open to any type of assistance that would level me up. We both knew that my organizational skills and focus were hurting. At the time, that was her expertise. I asked her for help and ended up enrolling in some of her workshops.

They were very helpful, and I have since implemented some of her ideas into my life and career.

One technique she suggested has stuck with me to this day. It is something I use and suggest to other people who have a lot on the go. She asked me to create a life spreadsheet. Carissa calls it "Creating a Better Version of Yourself." It is a way to track where you are spending your time and helps to ensure you are not overextending yourself when there isn't time to do so.

You start by listing the days of the week in a row along the top, and then all of the hours in a day in a column to the left. Then you document every minute of each day for a week. You note the time you go to bed, the time you wake up, the first thing you do in the morning, how long it takes to get dressed, make breakfast, drive to work, talk on the phone, scroll through social media. You enter your work hours, TV time, quality time with friends/family, etc. If you have business meetings or appointments with your personal trainer, you put them in. When I first did this exercise, I simply estimated the time it took for me to do each of these activities. At the end, I noticed that my totals averaged more than twenty-four hours per day, which was impossible. I was overbooked and dropping the ball left, right and centre—and now I had a visual that showed me why. I pared back on my activities and made sure I added a bit of buffer time for margin of error. After I was done, I had a realistic view of what an average week in my life was like.

The next part was the most powerful for me. If I wanted to do something new, begin a new project, or even a new leisure activity, I had to remove something from my spreadsheet. I had to take the item that meant the least to me and remove it in order to add something new. If I decided that I wanted to write a movie script and that I would devote an hour a day to this goal, something else had to give. Maybe I would restrict my Netflix time, or drinks with friends. Maybe I wanted to do something new, but I didn't want to give up anything else in my life at the time. If that was the case, I had to say *no* to the new thing, at least for the time being. Although I don't use the spreadsheet on a daily basis anymore, going through the exercise allowed me to create a new mental habit where I consider what comes in and what goes out before committing to anything new. By asking for help in an area where I needed it, I was able to level up and was given the opportunity to network with an entirely new group of people.

Moral of the story: A simple spreadsheet and a little self-awareness can have a big impact on how much you can achieve and enjoy your life.

Move It Forward

I discovered another important tool for keeping multiple projects on track while working as an executive producer with Mosaic Entertainment. Mosaic is a multi-platform company that has produced millions of dollars' worth of content. To run a successful production company you need to be able to manage many different projects at many different stages at the same time.

Every project in the pipe at Mosaic needed something different in order to move ahead. As a producer, it's easy to get distracted or caught up in one project and drop the ball on another. With many looming deadlines, meetings and boxes to check, you need a system to ensure you aren't missing anything and keep the whole train moving forward. One of my business partners had a strategy for doing just that. I call it the "Move It Forward" technique. It was so effective that I have used it on every project I have been a part of since.

Allow me to reintroduce the spreadsheet.

In this instance, the spreadsheet was on our office wall. We used chalk paint to draw a huge table where we could list everything we were working on every day. In columns and rows, we mapped out the names of the projects, the next steps and the proposed due dates. Different colours of chalk indicated the urgency of the next step. Green was low urgency, yellow was semi-urgent and red needed to be completed yesterday. As each task was completed, we'd erase it and then write in the next logical step along with a new due date.

What I love about this project-management technique is that it always gives me something to do. If I am overwhelmed by one task, I can look at the wall, consider the plethora of other tasks that need to be done and choose the one that excites me the most.

Once you start producing shows, many people will come to you with scripts and ideas, hoping you will be able to make their dream a reality. For any filmmakers or content creators out there, I'll share a trade secret for determining whether a project will be added to our slate: Two of the magical triad have to be in place: a great story, amazing attachments (cast, writer, director, etc.) and some level of funding. If a project fell on our lap that had two of those elements zipped up, we knew we could make it work. If it only had one, we would most likely pass. If a unicorn with all three ever came our way, we knew we had a home run.

The Move It Forward technique can also be thought of as a philosophy. No matter what passion project you've convinced yourself is for another lifetime, you can still make it happen in this one. Even if you don't know the exact path you need to take to reach your goal, I bet you *do* know what the next step is. Even if the end goal seems like it may be years away, you simply need to take the short view. Only look at what is next. Then put one foot in front of the other.

You want to write a book? Don't. Instead, write a paragraph, a sentence or an idea—but do it every day. You want to learn an instrument? Don't feel that you need to be good. You just need to be consistent. Pick up that instrument every day and make some noise. Make noise without judgment. Want a new career? Start by talking about it with everyone who will listen. Maybe your easiest next step is tightening up your resumé. Identifying the next step—the smaller the better—that causes the least amount of emotional pain is usually an amazing place to start.

13

KNOW WHEN TO
HOLD 'EM

"Everything is worth it. The hard work, the times when you're tired, the times where you're a bit sad . . . In the end, it's all worth it because it really makes me happy. There's nothing better than loving what you do."

—AALIYAH

K enny Rogers' song "The Gambler" says it best. Recognizing that the time has come to pack it in can be difficult. I am often an armchair investor when I watch *Shark Tank* or *Dragons' Den*, where hopeful entrepreneurs present their lifelong passion projects to the judges in the hopes of securing financing to take their enterprises to the next level.

Most of the time, I smile with pride as I watch people stand up for something they have created and that they believe is amazing. When they get it right, it brings tears to my eyes. I love seeing people achieve everything they set their minds to. Every once in a while, however, a hopeful entrepreneur hits the stage and asks for a large sum of money for a product that hasn't made any sales but the creator has already poured their life savings into. From my perspective, it's clear that they should have folded a long time ago.

I get the same feeling whenever I hear people refer to their project as their "baby." When something is your "baby" you'll do anything to give it a chance. You'll take out a second *and* third mortgage on your house, or sell all your belongings, just because you believe in your baby. Sure, some people have been successful taking this approach, but more often than not, tunnel vision creates major problems. It happens to the best of us. Some of the projects and businesses that I've started worked out great; others I now realize I should have folded or run away from. Knowing when to move and in which direction will save you a lot of stress, heartache and money.

ONE OF MY fitness companies, a boutique studio providing specialized personal training programs to people in all walks of life, was going through a tough spot. We had created a phenomenal environment of love and support in our space. The clients felt at home, and the staff felt like family. Running a small business is challenging at the best of times, but we had hit a point where it was getting hard to keep the lights on and ensure our staff were well paid. My business partner and I discussed all of our options, waffling between breaking our lease and closing shop or figuring out new ways to make more money fast. Our biggest problem at the time was that we couldn't pay ourselves and also pay all the bills. One of these expenses had to go, and we needed a quick influx of money. We decided to "hold 'em."

That decision meant that I would take a break from the company I had founded and run for over seven years at the time to sell cars. As you can imagine, most people who heard this thought I had lost my mind. But I knew a couple of things about myself: I was flexible and I was good at sales. I'd also heard that you could make upward of $30,000 per month selling cars, and that was the amount we needed to get our company back on track.

I know some of you are thinking *If you were so good at sales, why couldn't you make more money in the business you were in?* The answer is that our current space was too small to accommodate more clients and we needed the cash quickly in order to expand or get a bank loan.

Once I made the decision I wanted to be a car salesman, I walked confidently into a dealership that a friend suggested and told them I wanted to sell cars. I inquired about the earning potential, and they assured me that my numbers were accurate. For anyone who is unfamiliar with car sales, it runs 100 percent

THE ART OF DOING

on commission. If you are not selling cars, you are not making any money.

The boss sat me down, went over the basics, and gave me instructions on how to sell cars. This is where I learned a big lesson about myself: my ego can get in my way. I heard what my boss was telling me, but my internal monologue was saying *Yeah, yeah. I know how to sell. I'll just be me and people will buy.* I started halfway through the month so my sales target was seven to ten cars. I needed to sell thirty cars a month to save my fitness business. After doing things my way, I ended the first month with a grand total of 1.5 cars sold, earning just over $1000 when it was all said and done. I was gutted and just about ready to retire from car sales.

My boss pulled me into his office for a heart-to-heart about what happened. He asked if I had followed procedure, if I had followed his advice. I admitted that I hadn't because I didn't believe that it would work. His techniques were so simple and boring, the scripts were bland and had no character—I was convinced that surely what I was bringing to the table would fare better. I was wrong and made very little money. But instead of letting me go, my boss offered me an amazing deal. If I stayed and did everything he told me, paid attention to every detail and followed the process, I would make $30,000. He went a step further and promised that if I used all the techniques he recommended and didn't sell thirty vehicles, he would personally pay me $10,000. I mean, who could say no to a deal like that? I shook his hand and changed my strategy.

For the next month I did everything he instructed. I crossed my ts and dotted my is. I followed the scripts, made the calls, followed up on clients and everything in-between. By the end of the month, I'd sold thirty-three cars and made just over $30,000. To his surprise, I left the company. I had a bigger goal, but the lessons I learned while I worked there changed my life. The big three follow.

1. Trust the Process

Trust the process. I can't emphasize enough how important this is. I realize that those three words can be a challenge for many of us to follow. Generally speaking, there's a good reason why a process has been established and often it's accompanied by an instruction manual. The scientific method is a great example of a process. Based on the use of hypotheses and theories, it has helped humanity immensely. We trust the scientific model (well, most of us do), and we should apply that same trust when we are presented with a tried-and-true process. Sometimes, you learn about a proven process but decide that process may not work for someone like you. You find ways to tinker with it and adjust it so it fits better into your life. Then you find yourself unhappy with the results. You then decide that the entire undertaking was a waste of time because it didn't pan out the way you planned, even though you didn't follow the process.

Trusting the process can also apply to unknown futures. You may have set off on a path without a handbook or tutor.

Your gut and your passion pushed you in a specific direction and you listened. Only later you abort the journey because something didn't feel right or wasn't as smooth as you had envisioned. In these cases, I urge you to trust the process, go with the flow, and let your passion guide you to your destination. As long as you are moving with your goal in mind, trust, trust, trust the process.

The first time I tried selling cars, I didn't trust the process. I decided that I would cherry-pick the things I liked and make up the rest to suit my comfort level. I got a rude awakening when my results were sub-par. I wanted to pack it in and try something new. It wasn't until I fully committed myself to the process laid before me that I reaped the rewards.

Of course, once you have followed the steps and seen the process through to the end, some experimentation is encouraged. Now is the time to tinker and play. After you have a bigger picture of what is required, thanks to those who came before you, you can make the process your own and perhaps even make it more efficient for those who follow. It is a game of patience and discipline.

2. Sacrifice a Little to Gain a Lot

You have to give up a little to get a lot. What you give up will change depending on the situation at hand. Is it time, money, relationships, ego? Once you realize what it is, are you willing to give that thing up for the new want? These are questions we must ask ourselves before embarking on anything new.

Discipline is the key ingredient here. Are we willing to sacrifice short-term rewards for long-term gains? The sacrifices that we make today will help us realize the dream that our future self will get to enjoy. If we succumb to short-term quick hits of pleasure, the finish line of that dream keeps moving further away.

In high school, I was always envious of the kids who went to parties and hung out after school with their friends. I knew why I couldn't and so did they. The reason I wasn't allowed to go on school ski trips or go drinking at bush parties wasn't a secret. I was on a mission and that mission was clear from an early age. If I wanted to go to post-secondary school, I would have to earn a full scholarship. In order to earn a full scholarship, I would have to achieve a certain athletic standard and obtain a specific grade-point average.

Understanding the mission and living it are two different things. I often found myself looking through the window and wondering if I was missing something important. Was trading fun with my friends now for a potential payoff later worth it? Well, fast forward a few decades and I can tell you: damn right it was! Phew, am I glad I didn't succumb to the short-term shot-gunning of beers by the bonfire on the weekly in exchange for what hard work offered me.

Sometimes it can be hard to see the light at the end of the tunnel. It can feel like you have to do so much today for the chance of gaining something tomorrow. One of the strongest reframes I have ever employed is a simple one-word swap. I would catch myself saying *I have to do this* and *I have to do that*. By changing "have" to "get," everything transformed into a privilege. I *get* to go to work today. I *get* to look after my kids, watch them play sports, take care of them when they are sick, tuck them into bed and make them breakfast in the morning. I *get* to create new revenue streams and collaborate with friends on projects. I *get* to solve problems for a living. I *get* to follow the process. I get to, I get to, I get to . . . What an amazing life I get to live.

Working at the car lot, I had to sacrifice my free time, socializing with friends, my ego . . . I had to sacrifice it all. Let me state that differently: I got to sacrifice it all in order to put myself in the best position to win. It isn't so much about how bad you want something. The real question is: how long are you willing to suffer for it? Whether you want to save your fitness studio, make the NHL or win the Nobel Prize, you will have to endure some suffering. You might want to be an actor, but how many times are you willing to accept rejection? You might want to be the next country-music star, but how long are you prepared to sleep on someone's couch and give up other things you enjoy in life to get there? How long you are willing to suffer to get the life you want is a pretty accurate barometer of how bad you really want it.

You have to give up a little to get a lot.

3. That's It, That's All

Knowing when it is time to quit is paramount. Everything has a time—a start and a finish. Hanging on too long or for the wrong reasons creates an imaginary safety net that doesn't help us progress. The golden handcuffs you put on when you accept a large sum of money for a job you do not enjoy is a perfect example. Let me be very clear: I *hated* selling cars. It did not feed my soul at all. It was a means to an end. Some people love the profession and are built to do it for the long haul. I am not one of them. Of course, the money I was making at the time created a bit of a dilemma. I struggled with my initial plan to leave car sales to go back to a career that could barely afford me. I had to decide whether to take a massive pay cut so I could continue pursuing a passion that paid me in different ways. I wavered on this decision even though I knew my heart wasn't in the sales job. Ultimately, I made the correct choice for my life and ended up in a much happier and healthier position, where I flourished. I have seen many people make the wrong choice.

Many people are financially wealthy and miserable. I've learned from my few conversations with the uber rich that they usually weren't happy until they followed their passions. Of course it's easy to follow your passions when money isn't an issue. However, I've heard the same tune from people over and over, from all walks of life. Time and time again, all signs point to following that burning desire in your soul, regardless of financial gain.

If money is your be-all and end-all, I encourage you to find someone who is making a lot of it doing the very thing you are scared to do. They are out there to show you that it can be done, and it can be done by you. You just have to know when it's your time to make the leap.

The choice to leave the fitness studio to make some extra

money selling cars proved to be the correct decision for our business. However, it still took many years for the enterprise to run smoothly. Even with all the sweat and tears we put into it, there came a time when we needed to say "that's it, that's all." Our timing was good: one of our trainers expressed an interest in purchasing his own fitness studio, making it the perfect time for us to walk away. He bought our company and took it to bigger and better levels. A perfect end to a lesson-riddled stint in the fitness industry.

FlowPower is another fitness company I started with several business partners. It's designed to give people at any fitness level video instruction to take their fitness journey to the next level. No special equipment is needed. It's a simple but very effective fitness routine for everyone from couch potatoes to elite athletes. I spent many years creating the program and the nutrition guidelines that go along with it to make it efficacious overall.

My partners and I decided that we wanted to create high-quality videos that would stand the test of time. We wanted to battle on par with some of the heavy hitters in the online fitness space, including the Beachbodys of the world. In order to do this, we needed to raise a large sum of money to cover the production and marketing of the content.

After many years of planning, fundraising and execution, we completed the program. The next step was to get it in front of as many eyeballs as we could. We found a partner in California that had created successful marketing campaigns for many of the big players in the fitness video world. Everything was lining up for us to be the next big thing in home fitness videos.

And then the DVD bubble popped. Just as we invested our money creating a top-of-the-line infomercial that would play on cable networks all over North America, North America decided that digital assets would now lead the charge. In the blink of an eye, DVDs became a thing of the past and all of our marketing material driving people to purchase them became obsolete. Reality set in and we were left with a hard decision. We had an amazing product that we knew would sell, but we didn't have any money left to reconfigure our marketing strategies. The amount of reinvestment needed would be substantial, with no guarantee of success, and it could end up costing our investors much more than they had initially signed up for. Sure, that's the nature of business investments, but we cared about our investors and wanted to find a way to recoup their investment and ultimately make some money.

For several years my business partner and I tried to shift to a digital platform. We worked for free, trying to rebrand and sell our product any way we could. However, we lacked the capital, and, technology was sprinting away from us as we inched closer to a forgone conclusion. We knew it was time to focus our energies on other areas.

Whenever you walk away from something, it stings. You can't escape the bite, but you can take away some lessons if you are open to them. We learned that there are no sure things, that the quality of your product does not guarantee success, that relationships are on the line when you go into business with others, and that as long as you put your all into making it work, you can still walk away with your head held high. The wonderful thing about creating a top-notch product is that you never know when the market will shift and the thing you made may end up being the thing someone needs in the future (fingers crossed).

14

YOU GET TO KEEP TRYING

"I realized that beauty was not a thing that I could acquire or consume, it was something I just had to be."
—LUPITA NYONG'O

You are a creator. You were created by creators, and whether you have children or not, you will continue to create while you have breath in your body. A lot of people like to separate themselves into categories, believing that they are either pragmatic or creative. Some of those people also believe that you have to be born with creativity. However, I stand by the statement that we are all creators—it's in our blood.

Everything we do is a product, a creation, of our thoughts, our words and our actions. People get a little prickly when I tell them that the life they are living right now is the life they created with the tools they had at the time. Of course, external factors play a large part in our perceived lot in life, but you are the creator of the life you lead. Imagine your life is a movie script and you are the author. Every minute of every hour of every day, you get to pen your next move. Of course, consequences follow each decision, but those are ancillary to the movement you create with your next step.

If you need creative inspiration from free-thinking individuals, visit any elementary school or playground and you will see it in action. Finger painting, family drawings, popsicle-stick art are all beautiful examples of creativity in motion. My wife and I watch our youngest son, age seven, play make-believe for hours. After pushing back on not being allowed to watch any more screens, he'll immerse himself in his own virtual reality for hours at a time. The world we live in melts away as he narrates scenes and gives voices to characters engaged in an epic battle. He'll create all the sound effects and the musical score to add intensity. It is a beautiful thing to behold. Our son and countless other children out there have the ability to create a world within a world that feels every bit as real as the one we are in right now. They understand that they are the screenwriters of their next moments. It's only when adults step in and start making edits and re-writes to their magical journey that they come back to the fray. Then things start to change. Those same children begin to behave differently. Their creative spark begins to diminish as outside influences, parental expectations and internal beliefs change. Some of us, the lucky ones, find a way to nourish that creative side of ourselves. We put time and energy into dreaming when the world tells us that our dreams play second fiddle to more analytical activities. Still, some of us found a way to thrive in that space and grew up to be what many now call artists and creators. For those folks who didn't consent to have their creativity slowly drained from them, it's time to fill up and feel that maker energy again.

Adopting new ways of thinking and behaving is hard. Once we get comfortable in our habits and routines, it's difficult to introduce new ones. A lot of the time, we are scared. We are scared to start because we are scared to fail. On paper, we understand that "failure" is a natural part of life, but when faced with the reality of failure we rarely embrace it. I put the word "failure" in quotations because I don't believe we ever really fail at doing something. I believe we have two options: we quit or we die. When we "fail" at something, we've just decided it is over. Let's say we applied for a new job and were rejected. We may take that as a failure, but, in reality, we can apply again. We can choose to try again and again and again until we decide we want to pivot and change direction. Or maybe we started a painting and it didn't turn out the way we had envisioned. Did we fail or did we complete an attempt? Many of my own paintings, my favourite ones, are products of many completed attempts on the same canvas. It is those attempts, after some time and distance, that give me perspective on what I ultimately end up with on that canvas. When I say you can't fail at something, I mean you get to keep trying until you take your last breath.

If we are going to use the word *failure*, we need to rethink our relationship with it and better understand how to leverage it to create more wins in our life. A successful failure is when you push your limits and find the edges of what is comfortable. To put it plainly, it is becoming comfortable being uncomfortable. The first step in finding successful failures is doing. You have to do *before* you feel ready to do it. Getting ready wastes so much valuable do time. Preparation is always important, but when preparation turns into fearful procrastination, we end up doing ourselves a major disservice. I was lucky enough to get real-world perspective on successful failures when I was a professional athlete.

As a professional high jumper, I wasn't allowed to win until I lost. I had to knock the bar down three times before the competition was over. Regardless of whether I finished in first or last place, I was required to try my best and fail three times before I could obtain my official result. The notion that I had to test my limits not once, not twice, but three times before I was able to assess my performance was ingrained. I spent most of my athletic life training to find the edges and limits of what I could do on any given day. Finding those edges and then being brave enough to try my hardest was a prerequisite. It didn't matter how I felt; I had to locate those uncomfortable limits and test them. Make no mistake, when I am faced with activities I am destined to fail at, I am petrified and want to turn back. But that fearful feeling has become addictive. I'm addicted to finding failure in my life because I have seen the predictive outcome of positivity that lies on the other side, every time.

As we age we search for comfort. This makes sense, as most of us battled to finish school, to find a partner, to get a career, to have a family, etc., all in an effort to build a comfortable life.

Searching for uncomfortable situations may seem counterintuitive, but watch what happens when you place a crawling baby in a yard. Once they get the courage to explore, they will venture to find the edges of their environment. They'll try to see how far they can go and, usually, won't turn around until a guardian pulls them back to safety. As we get older, we stop looking for those edges and we get complacent in our yards.

In order to create the best life you can, you must also be on the lookout for failure. You must undertake a diligent quest to find failure and embrace it as the teacher it always is. Failure then becomes a beacon. It directs us to a place where we can narrow our attention and level up whatever it is we were attempting.

Actors are very comfortable with failure. The job inevitably includes a string of rejections. It can be a real bummer. Imagine being turned down for a job interview that you have put your heart and soul into. Now imagine doing that three to five times a week, every month of every year. Actors are already sensitive souls, often needing external validation. You either get used to repeated rejection or you find another vocation. People often question why we put ourselves through it. It's because we know the big ups that live on the other side of the many downs. With each rejection, we learn. With every *no* our fire intensifies and we search for ways to level up at the next opportunity. We may not know why casting makes their decisions, but we always know we can be better next time.

When I am speaking, I often ask people to raise their hand if they have ever contemplated writing a book or a movie script or learning a new instrument or language. I watch as a bunch of hands hesitantly rise in the air. I then ask everyone to look around the room to see how many other people shared their desires. Then I ask them to keep their hand up if they have done it. By "done it" I mean have published the book, produced the screenplay, learned the new instrument or become proficient in another language. With each clarifying question, hands slowly lower. By the end of the question period only a fraction of hands remain. We applaud the doers in the room who found a way to see their passion through to the end. Then I turn to discovering the underlying truths of why so many people dropped their hand. Usually people still-wanted to achieve these things, but years had passed and they realized that they hadn't even taken the next step to make their goal happen. Of course they wanted this; they thought about it all the time. But they couldn't figure out why they couldn't get going.

We all have goals in mind—large, small and somewhere in-between. We may not reach them all. Sometimes on our way to one place, we end up at another failure. Depending on our mindset, that failure might be where we were always meant to be. It's about the journey, not the destination. I had the pleasure of meeting and hearing a speaker who made that age-old saying hit harder than ever before.

Every once in a while a speaker says something that can change your life. For me, this was Mike Dooley, a *New York Times* bestselling author, speaker and entrepreneur in the New Thought movement. I attended one of his presentations and later met with him to discuss his work. His teachings contain the premise that our thoughts become things.

Everything starts with a thought—the shirt you are wearing, the laptop you work on, the chair you are sitting in all began with a single thought. Someone thought about it, wrote something down, made a plan, maybe found some investors, followed through on their plan, marketed their product, sold the idea and now people pay for that actualized thought. Thoughts are so powerful. My mom and dad looked at each other, had a thought and—boom-chicka-wow-wow—nine months later I arrived: my parents' real, live thought experiment. (Thanks, Monica and Richard, for having . . . those kinds of thoughts on that night.)

Dooley's words hit me like an epiphany. I've followed the idea that a person can manifest anything they want, but it never landed in such a concrete way until I heard Dooley explain it. I was giddy with excitement. I felt as though I'd been given a secret key.

Whether or not you subscribe to the notion that you can create anything with a thought doesn't matter. You don't need to believe in a fact for it to be true. The life you are currently leading is designed by you, mostly by your subconscious. Dooley's words reminded me that I am in the driver's seat, a place we all operate from.

Dooley spoke of a "universal GPS," which also resonated with me. The idea is that you input your desired goal, dream or passion into a mental GPS program just as you'd enter a destination on your phone. You think about where you want to go and you act on it, you type it into your navigation system. If you are parked when you enter your destination, the program will give you an estimated time of arrival and the distance to your end point. It doesn't give you any real-time information until you move.

Most of us do not study the GPS map or memorize each upcoming turn. We trust the program and pay attention to the next direction. The only thing the GPS needs is for you to input the goal and move. If you keep moving, you keep getting new instructions. Life throws us curve balls and sometimes we change course mid-journey. I might be headed to Seattle from Vancouver but then, thirty minutes into the trip, I feel my belly start to grumble. I don't stop the navigation process because I am making a pitstop at Popeyes for chicken. I trust that the GPS will give me revised instructions once I change direction. If it says turn left and I go right, GPS might prompt *Make a U-turn?* or *Rerouting*. Neither the GPS in my phone nor the universal GPS worry about detours or pit stops along the way. As long as we have decided where we want to go and continue making moves with that in mind, we will get there.

You want to be a painter? Great, make the choice and add movement. Movement might be a trip to the art store for supplies or it might be a trip to a gallery for inspiration. If you find yourself lacking creativity one day, don't be discouraged: Universal GPS knows where you are headed. Just keep moving.

Do you need a pitstop? Take one, but make sure you get back on the road with the same destination in mind. The worst thing you can do is get caught up in the perceived length of the journey or how much faster another person's car is or how much better you think other people's art might be. This is the point when some people decide to abandon the journey they were initially excited about and input another destination into their GPS. Or maybe they don't bother with the GPS anymore and choose to travel familiar roads without any directional help. What a sad tale it would be to never travel outside of your neighbourhood when there is an entire planet to experience. Get the canvas, paint, make a mess. Get in the car and trust that you'll arrive as long as you are moving. It doesn't matter what you want to create or what it looks like, once you have decided you want it, put it in the universal GPS and start moving.

THERE IS NO other you. You are perfectly unique. No one can do it like you do it. You are a unicorn! Why not be the best unicorn? Why not embrace all the weirdness, the bizarreness and the quirks that make you an original? Comparing yourself to others is silly because they'll never have what you have, know what you know or be able to deliver the same product the way you can. Lean in and refine yourself until you are proud of the person staring back at you in the mirror. You might look different than the next person, you might think in different ways and you might move differently than them—that's great! That is what will make you stand out. You may have gone through things that no one else will ever understand. All of these things make you special and original. Some people use these differences as crutches, as reasons why they can't. I urge you to look at them as reasons why you can, why you should.

As I've said from the start, *The Art of Doing* is not a passive book. It requires you to do, and do a lot. Some people say that life is short. I say that life is the longest thing you'll ever experience. You have more time than you realize to do all the things you have dreamed of. The only thing you don't have time for is waiting or believing that your moment has passed.

Hurry up and get your first thing done. It doesn't matter if it is your first book, song or speech. It's highly probable that it will be one of the worst things you'll do. It may be good, but compared to your market average it's more likely to be one of your worst versions. That's okay. You are only going to get better with time and each attempt, so why wait? Get the crappy stuff out of the way so you can make awesomeness. Seize the moment.

DID YOU SEE that? Another moment just passed you by. Look at all those moments waiting for you to grab them and start moving and doing. By now you know that the road isn't going to be paved in gold. It may not be paved at all. You might have to clear the brush or excavate your way forward, but who cares? Don't wait. Take that first step, make that first move, do it all! You have the tools you need to master The Art of Doing. And the best time to start is now.

EPILOGUE

*"There's a certain amount of fearlessness
to not be afraid to speak your truth."*
—MC LYTE

The irony of this book is that I was stuck in that all-too-familiar place of inaction and fear for several months before I could start writing. I found myself lying in my bed, day after day, staring at the walls, trying to motivate myself to open my computer and get back to this project. Writer's block isn't anything new nor are rapidly approaching deadlines, and neither seem to elicit motivation. Being *The Art of Doing* guy also comes with its own set of expectations. I thought, *Who am I to pen a book about productivity if I contemplate scrapping the whole thing because of insecurities, external pressures or real-life stressors?*

The fact is I was having a hard time and I was struggling to *do*. I know many of us have been faced with different hurdles that we needed to jump over in order to complete a project. However, I was facing something new. An unforeseen turn of events was taking a toll on my self-confidence, my self-esteem and my ability to see the light at the end of the tunnel.

A wrecking ball had just smashed into my life and was threatening to damage everything I had ever created: I was on bail after being charged with a crime I did not commit.

Let me say that again for the people in the back: *I was officially on bail and formally charged with a very serious crime.*

That charge has now been fully withdrawn, but when I started writing this book my future was in the hands of a system that historically has not served people who look like me. The fallout from this event shook much of what I used to believe was true. I questioned my faith in friends, in people and even in myself. At the same time, making a commitment to myself and this book allowed me to use the tools I write about to get to the finish line.

As a 6'4", 265 lb.-Black man, it has been my intention to never find myself fingerprinted or behind the lens for a mug shot. I am well aware of the disproportionate negative outcomes for Black and brown people navigating many of the systemically racist systems that are currently in full operation. The odds were not stacked in my favour. The realities of these inequities have been ingrained in me from a very young age. From statistics to my own lived experience, I have seen the system fail many people of colour. Regardless of my innocence, my fear was founded.

As I was going through this painful time, I couldn't help but remember the "talk" my parents had given me when I was a child. "The talk" is the conversation many Black parents have with their children about racial inequities and how to navigate a world that may see you as a threat solely for the colour of your skin. It is statistically proven that Black boys are seen as older and more of a threat than lighter-skinned boys by many people in positions of authority. I was given the typical instructions: Be respectful if law enforcement stops you, keep your hands where they can see them, don't wear hoods. Stay out of trouble because if trouble ever arises, you will be the person they remember.

I can still hear my mother telling me how I needed to behave in elementary school. Not only did I have to behave, I had to behave better than my friends who didn't share the same skin colour as me. She said, "If a fight breaks out in the school yard, it doesn't matter if you were in it or not. Everyone will remember that Jesse was there." She was reminding me that my little Black face would be remembered in a sea of White ones. As a result, I needed to be mindful of my own actions and those of the people in my immediate vicinity. I needed to do more than others to steer clear of trouble because it would most certainly stick to me.

I was doing so well. Forty-some years of life without a run-in and BOOM, everything changed on May 6, 2022.

To sum it up, a person was injured at my residence. Shortly after the incident, that person proceeded to tell a tale to the police, a story of violence and assault. Each day this fable continued, it became more and more unbelievable. Initially, I couldn't wrap my head around the idea that a story so absurd was being taken seriously. Then I started to hear rumours circulating. I was reading messages online and hearing second-hand reports of people talking around the city. Everything crystallized into a very real problem when I was asked to turn myself in at a police station.

It was a nightmare. At no point did I think the police would believe the story being told to them. Nor did I think that it would culminate in me being booked into a downtown police station in Edmonton. I was dead wrong. Many months later, I was in a police station and my rights were being read to me. Shortly after that, I was ushered down the hall to get my fingerprints and mug shots taken.

As if this humiliation wasn't enough, a month later an article titled "Edmonton Actor Charged with Aggravated Assault" was published. The principle that the accused is considered innocent until proven guilty had never felt more antiquated than it did then. I may have been innocent until proven guilty in a court of law, but minds were already made up in the court of public opinion.

The solid reputation I had garnered over the decades from speaking to schools and businesses was in tatters. Never mind that I'd never fought, I don't yell and I couldn't remember a time

I'd ever lost my temper. People no longer had confidence in me. They cancelled contracted events and postponed future gigs. Even film and television bookings were slipping through my hands as a result of this unfounded charge. Everything felt out of control. I felt like I couldn't hold onto anything. My ability to exist in the life and career I had constructed seemed like it was slipping away. I was at the mercy of time, opinion and the system. The last thing I wanted to do was open my laptop and write a book with tips and tricks to motivate folks chasing their dreams while mine were being ripped away from me—or so I thought.

And then it hit me: This is *exactly* the time to write this book! It's one thing to rehash strategies I have used in the past to get through difficult spots, but it's quite another to stare a big problem in the face and utilize the teaching moments to march my way through in real time. My particular situation may have been unique, but the size of my problem wasn't. Whether you are dealing with one or two major life stressors or several small ones, they all take their toll and they all need to be dealt with in a similar fashion.

Fortunately, the charges were eventually withdrawn and I never had to prove anything in court. The weight I had been feeling for a full year began to lift, and I was able to start the process of clearing my name and get back to the real, meaningful work that I loved to do. Thankfully, I was able to remain focused and creative during one of the most stressful periods of my life.

Our own expectations, the fear of failing and letting ourselves and others down, the pressure other people place on us—these are all excuses we make for not starting the project of our dreams. These may also be the reasons why we can't seem to finish the things we've started. We find ways to justify why we haven't checked off our bucket-list items. We create excuses for pushing off mundane day-to-day tasks. We harbour disappointment when we find ourselves failing at everything from learning a new instrument, starting a new career, missing a social gathering or simply returning a text late. All of these tasks can seem insurmountable without the right tools.

The tools you need are outlined in this book. They are the exact tools you'll require to achieve greatness on any scale. You'll have them at hand when you finally decide that you are no longer willing to travel down the same old path and are ready to embrace something new and exciting.

Once you decide to actively participate in learning and using the tools in this book, getting things done will no longer feel like an unbearable weight. It will begin to lighten until it has become an art—The Art of Doing.

THE
ART OF DOING
PLAYBOOK

The Art of Doing may be the least passive reading experience you'll ever have. Work through the tools in this Playbook after you have finished reading the chapters. You can use the tools as many times as you want and for as many projects or goals as you wish to complete. My words alone can't do the work for you, but the twenty-four tools in this Playbook can help you get started. Making small changes can lead to big results—but you already knew that.

Ain't no time like the present. Are you ready to leap?

THE TOOLS

1

GROW YOUR ADAPTABILITY AND RESILIENCE

Maintaining momentum despite setbacks or obstacles as you work toward your goals requires resilience and adaptability. In this section you will need to spend some time journaling and writing lists.

TOOL 1:
REFRAME YOUR OBSTACLES AS OPPORTUNITIES

Think of the obstacles you are facing in your life right now. Can you reframe them as opportunities? How can you use your obstacles to create freedom in your future? For example, if money is an obstacle now, how can you save, fundraise, collaborate, etc. to keep this obstacle from getting in the way in the future? Sometimes the obstacle is so close that we can't see a way through. Back up, reframe and try to find another way around. Spend some time writing in your journal, brainstorming roadmaps around your current obstacles and/or reframing them as opportunities to get you closer to your destination.

TOOL 2:

SURROUND YOURSELF WITH A SUPPORTIVE NETWORK

Identify your support system—these should be people who can provide you with different perspectives, solutions, and emotional support when things get tough. Once you know who they are, ask them to be a part of your team. Then share your goals and challenges. Most people want to see you succeed and would love to be a part of that success. Seek advice, encouragement and feedback. Additionally, consider appointing an accountability partner who can help you stay on track and provide motivation, especially during challenging times.

It isn't uncommon to want to cower and hide in a hole when the going gets tough, so you'll want to ensure you have a strong support system you can lean into. More people are in your corner than you think!

2

LOVE YOUR DIRECTION

When we repeat actions consistently, we create habits, both good and bad. Once you start running toward love consistently, you'll begin to form positive habits that you can apply to all areas of your life every day. The following tools are just to get you started. Try one or all of them. If it resonates with you, give it a go.

TOOL 3:
FIND YOUR LOVE

Make a list of the top five things you love to do. Ideally, these should be activities that can be done alone and require very little input or participation from anyone else. Once you have your list, circle your favourite three things. When you are feeling stuck, these three activities will help you reset by giving you quick dopamine hits. (My top three are drawing, singing and writing.)

TOOL 4:
FIND YOUR FEAR

Identify the key area(s) in your life where fear still has a hold on you. It can be a fear that is preventing you from getting started or the guiding factor behind what you are doing. Once you have identified your fear, imagine a world where fear doesn't exist. How different would your world look? Now write an impact statement outlining how this fear has controlled or affected your life and what it would look like if it weren't there. The act of visualizing a different reality than the one you are living can offer insight and direction into how to bring it to fruition.

Use the following two fill-in-the-blank sentences to create your impact statement. If more than one fear is holding you back, complete this exercise multiple times, once for each fear. Write your impact statements on sticky notes and place them somewhere you can see them every day.

First, fill in the blanks:

I would love to _____ if _____ wasn't in the way.

Then, reframe the sentence, filling in the blanks with your intended action:

I will _____ and _____ can't stop me.

3

PRACTICE SAYING *YES*

Practice makes permanent. Integrate the following tools into your daily life. The more you practice them, the more permanent the results will be. Use your journal to record when and how these tools impacted your day.

TOOL 5: SAY *YES*

This may be the easiest tool to put into practice: Say *yes* more often. Say *yes* to new experiences that come your way. If your snap reaction is to say *no*, pause and ask yourself *What amazing things could come from me saying* yes *in this moment?*

Remember: Saying *yes* more doesn't mean saying *yes* to everything. It's about being open to new experiences and opportunities that align with your values and goals while managing your commitments effectively.

When you do say *yes* to something new, take note of what experiences and opportunities came from this decision. Not all *yesses* are paved in gold; try to focus on the good that would not have existed had you remained in the *no* mentality.

TOOL 6:

CHANGE YOUR MINDSET
AND STAY FLEXIBLE

Cultivate a positive and open mindset that is willing to embrace new experiences. Be open to unexpected opportunities that may not align perfectly with your plans but could lead to growth and learning. Practice being adaptable and flexible by saying *yes* to opportunities that initially may not have been on your radar.

Don't be afraid to initiate the new *yesses* by asking yourself questions you have said *no* to in the past. For example, you might have been the person who always said *no* to going for a hike, playing pickleball or cooking a new dish. Instead, try to be the instigator in those circumstances. If you're able, include your team or accountability partner in these new activities.

TOOL 7:

CREATE A MINDFUL RISK ASSESSMENT

Before saying *yes*, take a moment to assess the potential risks and benefits of the opportunity. Consider the potential outcomes and whether the opportunity aligns with your values, goals and current commitments. While it's important to step out of your comfort zone, thoughtful consideration can help you make informed decisions that are in your best interests.

4

GET COMFORTABLE BEING UNCOMFORTABLE

Stepping out of your comfort zone and embracing vulnerability can lead to personal growth and meaningful experiences. Here are three tangible tools to help you achieve this.

TOOL 8:
CREATE AN EXPOSURE PLAN

Start by taking small steps outside of your comfort zone. Gradually expose yourself to situations that make you feel slightly uncomfortable but are manageable. This could involve speaking up in meetings, trying a new activity, or engaging in a social event. As you become more accustomed to dealing with small challenges, you'll build confidence in handling larger ones. My personal favourite baby-stepper is karaoke.

TOOL 9:
CREATE A BUSINESS PLAN FOR YOUR LIFE

As discussed in Chapter 4, creating a business plan for your life can add an immense amount of clarity to your future. Start by writing a mission statement for your life in your journal. A mission statement or a vision statement is an expression of your core values and your purpose. It should be short and to the point—one or two sentences about what you will do, how you'll do it and why. Next, list your core values. These will be reflected in your mission statement, but try to go a bit deeper here. Lastly, create a S.W.O.T (strengths, weaknesses, opportunities and threats) analysis for your life. The point of this exercise is to allow you to look at your life from an analytical perspective. This will allow you to be objective about the direction you want to take while taking into consideration all of the variables available to you today and in the future. Here's my mission statement, as an example:

JESSE LIPSCOMBE INC.
Mission Statement: To connect with humans in true and meaningful ways and to create art in any and every way that I am inspired to.
Core Values: G.L.A.C.E.*—Grace, Love, Authenticity, Creativity and Energy
*I love using acronyms to help me remember my core values.

S.W.O.T. Analysis:

Strengths: *Optimistic, Risk-taker, Patient, Forgiving, Competitive*

Weaknesses: *Disorganized, Procrastinator, Inconsistent, Impulsive*

Opportunities: *Leading groups, Inspiring/motivating, Big-picture planning*

Threats: *Mundane/repetitive tasks, Solitary work environments, Too much rope*

Once you have completed this assignment, use it to ensure that all of the activities you are spending your time on are truly ones that fit into the life you are trying to create. This exercise will also help direct you to the things that need to be eliminated from your life, the things that are not serving the larger plan you have outlined for yourself.

TOOL 10:
REFLECT

Write in your journal every day. Try to make a habit of it. Your entries do not need to be long—the simple act of reflecting on the things you have done each day will keep you accountable to the life you are creating. Write down your fears, challenges and successes. Let yourself be vulnerable. Reflect on your experiences, noting how each step outside of your comfort zone contributed to your personal growth. Over time, this record will serve as a reminder of your progress and the positive outcomes that come from embracing change.

5

EMBRACE POSSIBILITY

Look up when opportunities arise. Ask yourself *What if I gave this thing a go? What good could come from it?* By no means am I suggesting that you derail a well-thought-out plan every time something shiny comes along. Rather, I am asking you to be flexible enough to consider new options while you are on your path. The following two tools will help you with that process.

TOOL 11:
REACH OUT TO REACH IN

Pick someone who has been very influential in your life, someone who created an opportunity for you that shaped who you are today in a positive way. Once you have that person in mind, reach out to them and have a conversation about their life. Ask them what they did to get to where they are, what were some key decisions they made that resulted in them achieving their current status? In your journal, ask yourself the following questions and write down your answers: What would have happened if they didn't make some of those choices? Who would they be? Who would you be without their influence?

TOOL 12:
VISUALIZE AND MARINATE

Imagine a new opportunity falling in your lap today, something big and exciting. Visualize all the details. Then ask yourself what would happen if you chose to look up and follow it. Think of all of the new and positive things that might happen in your life. How would your life change? Sit in that feeling, get used to it and be ready to look to the skies the next time life drops your potential next step in front of your feet. The act of visualization helps our brain get used to the feeling of winning. Professional athletes use visualization on the daily to help re-wire our brains to feel comfortable in the place we want to be. Marinate in the juices of victory until it seeps into every pore of your being.

6

KNOW YOUR *WHY*

Understanding your *why* is crucial to building a strong foundation you can stand on as you build your dream and navigate challenges and obstacles. It plays an important role in determining and upholding a business's values. It also acts as your compass when starting a new career or project. When you know your *why*, you can always return to it if you find yourself off track or without focus. Knowing your *why* comes in handy when you are faced with unexpected roadblocks on the way to your ultimate destination. The following tools will help you uncover your *why* when embarking on new endeavours.

TOOL 13:
ASSESS YOUR PERSONAL VALUES

Identify and define your core values and then write them in your journal. If you have already completed your life's business plan, use this tool to flesh out your core values. If not, this tool is still effective on its own.

Your values represent what matters most to you in life. When embarking on a new project, consider how it aligns with your values. Ask yourself:

How does this project reflect my values?

Will this project contribute to something I deeply care about?

Does this project resonate with my sense of purpose?

TOOL 14:
ASK *WHY?* FOUR TIMES

The Four Whys is an established problem-solving technique used to explore the root cause of a given situation. Consider your goal and then ask *why?* four times, each time probing deeper into your motivations. For example:

Why am I starting this project? (Reason 1)

Why is that important to me? (Reason 2)

Why do I want to achieve Reason 2? (Reason 3)

Why will achieving this make my life better? (Reason 4)

By the time you reach the fourth *why?*, you've likely uncovered a more profound and meaningful *why?* that goes beyond surface-level motivations.

This tool will help you uncover the real motivations behind what you are after. For example, you may want to get a personal trainer because you want to lose weight (Reason 1). You may state that it is important to you because you want to fit into a specific bathing suit or look good for wedding pictures (Reason 2). You may follow that up by saying that you have looked at pictures of yourself in a bathing suit and felt self-conscious and that you don't like that feeling (Reason 3). After some thought, you may feel that losing weight will make your life better because you'll be tackling your insecurities and elevating your confidence (Reason 4). After completing this exercise, you will be able to use the more powerful *why?* you uncovered (becoming more confident and crushing your insecurities) as your fuel to keep going. This is a much stronger driver than wanting to lose a few pounds or fitting into a new bathing suit.

7

GRANT PERMISSION

Once we remember that we can give ourselves permission to do anything, we give ourselves real power. Use the following tool to help you take control of your life. Refer back to Chapter 8 to revisit some examples of where granting yourself permission can be helpful.

TOOL 15:
GIVE YOURSELF PERMISSION

Give yourself permission to do something. It could be permission to laugh more or permission to win. Or perhaps, next time you are out with friends and you hear a good song, give yourself permission to get up and dance, regardless of who is looking and who joins in. Whatever it is, grant yourself permission to try it. Pick something that really resonates with where you are currently in your life. Once you do it, pay attention to how much that one allowance affected your life. Later, take out your journal and document the experience. Repeat this exercise once a week (or as many times as you feel is beneficial), granting yourself permission for something else.

I've given you permission to try, but you have to give yourself permission to follow through. You're the boss now.

8

BE CURIOUS

Curiosity pushes us beyond our limiting beliefs and drives us into new experiences. It helps us find creative solutions to overcome the challenges in our lives. By simply opening yourself up and being inquisitive, you'll open yourself up to new and exciting possibilities. The doing part comes in when you decide to act on them. The following exercises will help you initiate a curious mindset.

TOOL 16:
EMBRACE BOREDOM

Take a twenty-four- to forty-eight-hour moratorium from all the things that distract you from being bored. Sit in your boredom and let your mind wander. After the initial struggle with wanting to reach for a typical dopamine fix (usually our phone and TV), you'll be able to create new outlets for your boredom. Embracing boredom allows us to transfer the time we used to use for mindless scrolling or watching re-runs to new activities that fit into our life's business plan and reflect our core values. Replace doom-scrolling with learning a new instrument or language. Shift the time you spend watching TV to time spent painting abstracts or planting and tending a garden. The choices are abundant once we break out of our typical boredom patterns.

TOOL 17:
DO THE DOODLE

Grab a blank piece of paper and something to draw with. Start doodling without expectation. See where your mind takes your hand. Without judgment or planning, just make a mess. Creating for the sake of creating (without a goal in mind) helps us to embrace to beauty of doing for the sake of doing. The goal here is to exercise a different part of your brain so the part that formerly saw a blank piece of paper and a pen now sees only possibility.

TOOL 18:
JUST JOURNAL

If you don't already, start journaling. Write about your day or week and how it made you feel. Give yourself a chance to download everything you are thinking. If you are stressed about work and family, write it down. If you are excited or nervous about an upcoming engagement, put it down on paper. Sometimes a journal can act like a great friend ready to listen to your every thought. Think about how you want your life to turn out. Imagine what you want your life to look like and write it down in as much detail as you can.

Writing down your thoughts is therapeutic in itself, but it also creates space for more exciting things to flourish in your brain. The act of journaling keeps you accountable to yourself and creates a written record of the promises you've made to yourself and the steps you've been taking toward them.

If you are new to journaling, try to do it daily. I like to journal in the morning, but find a time that works best for you.

9

VISUALIZE YOUR ACTUALITY

Visualization is a very strong tool that can prepare your mind and body for upcoming challenges and events in which you want to perform well. It's something I have practised for most of my athletic and performative career. Find a quiet place where you can be alone with your thoughts, and then give this visualization tool a try.

TOOL 19:
SEE IT TO ACHIEVE IT

In this exercise, I want you to recall a tough spot in your life when you felt all hope was lost. Perhaps it's an abusive relationship, a horrible job, an accident, or the loss of a loved one. Remember a time when you felt there was no light at the end of the tunnel. Now I want you to think about how you got through it.

Often we choose to forget the harder times in our life and bury them away. But when we block them out, we also block out all the things we did to survive. It's important to remember the people who helped you, the music that inspired you, the tactics you took to hold it all together. *It's important that you recognize that you made it.* Not only did you make it, but you came out of it with real tools that will help you if you ever face something as dire as that again in the future.

Whether you realize it or not, your toolkit has been getting bigger and more useful every day. All you have to do is claim those tools as your own so you can walk into whatever is coming for you with the confidence that you are already prepared and you will come out on top.

10

FAIL YOUR WAY TO VICTORY

Most people consider sucking at something a hallmark of an unenjoyable experience. We take up this habit when we are in elementary school and decide, for example, whether we are a math or English kind of person. If we score well on math tests, we end up saying that we love math. If we don't, we generally decide we are "not a math person" and stick with that narrative for the rest of our life. We always seem to run the other way once we discover we are under-performing in some area. In order to change that mindset, we need to reframe failure. One way to do that is to commit to doing something you are not proficient at. These tools will help you step confidently into things you suck at, and allow you to uncover the gold in failing.

TOOL 20:
FIND YOUR FAIL

Think of something that you have shied away from doing because you suck at it. Next, set aside some time to do that activity without much preparation. Just do it. Embrace the suck. Keep practising over days and weeks until you have a handle on it. Then try another sucky thing. Maybe even find a friend or a partner to suck at something with. You'll discover the joy in learning as well as new things you may have previously passed up that bring positivity into your life. Sucking at something means you have to push the edges of your comfort zone, forcing inner growth regardless of the outcome of the task.

11

THE BUSINESS OF LIFE

Are there things in your life that you are holding onto for the wrong reasons? Do you have a job that pays you well financially but drains you in every other way? Do you have a partner that you stay with because of their potential and not because of who they are now? Do you have a toxic friend that you only keep around because of how long you've known them? Take a look at your life and decide if it's time to walk away from something that no longer serves you in a positive way. Knowing when to hold on to something and when to let it go can be challenging. These three tools can help you navigate this decision-making process.

TOOL 21:
COMPLETE A
COST–BENEFIT ANALYSIS

Identify a situation that no longer serves you. Make a list of the benefits and drawbacks associated with holding on to or letting go of the situation in question. Be specific and objective about the positives and negatives, and then rank them in order of their importance to you.

Doing this should provide clarity on whether the benefits of holding on to that situation outweigh the benefits of letting go, or vice versa.

Next, give yourself a specific time frame (for example, a week or a month) to reflect on your decision. During this period, actively assess your feelings. Take note of any changes in your perspective, emotions, or circumstances. At the end of the reflection period, you'll have a better sense of whether your initial inclination to hold on or let go still holds true.

Sometimes, we make rash decisions based on our emotions instead of allowing ourselves time to marinate in the entirety of the situation and sift through the facts. Give yourself space to make the correct choice so you can move forward without regret.

TOOL 22:
FIND YOUR TRUSTED ADVISERS AND GET FEEDBACK

In the face of any big decision, gather advice from trusted friends, family members, mentors, or professionals who have experience or knowledge in the area or situation in which you are struggling. An outside perspective can shed light on aspects you may not have considered. Note that it's important to garner input from a diverse range of sources so you end up with a well-rounded view. At the end of the day, you have to make the final call, but considering outside perspectives will make sure you do it thoughtfully and methodically without getting caught up in too much emotion.

BONUS TOOLS

INTEGRATE EMOTION AND LOGIC

When considering the pros and cons of any situation, it can help to make a chart or a list that separates the emotional aspects from the logical ones. Grab a piece of paper and divide it into two columns. At the top of each column, fill in one of each heading: *Hold* and *Walk away*. Under each heading, list the emotional reasons to do each. Then list the logical reasons for both options. Review your list. Is one column more heavily weighted than the other?

Completing this exercise can help you appreciate the situation from multiple angles and, therefore, make a more balanced decision that draws up both your emotions and rational thinking.

GET UNSTUCK AND
MOVE FORWARD

Implement the Big Littles (page 156) and Move It Forward (page 165) strategies on your next project, or apply them to an ongoing project that might be stalled. If you are having difficulty keeping all of your tasks in order or feel stuck, these two tools will help jump-start your momentum.

DOER PROFILES

The Art of Doing is for everyone. To showcase how the tools in this book have influenced other people just like you, I have included a few profiles of folks that have put them to use. As you read their stories, start to visualize how yours will sound when you commit to making an art out of doing it all.

BOMBS TO BELTING

In 2020 I met Damian Radcliffe, director of operations for a security firm with a large footprint in the downtown Edmonton area. He and I were exploring how to help security professionals improve their interactions with marginalized individuals and the community at large. There'd recently been some troubling interactions between security personnel and some of the city's unhoused population. Radcliffe asked me to come in to brainstorm some new directions, help educate workers and collaborate on how the security field could do better for the people they serve and protect. We started by filming a series of "talking head" videos that he would circulate to his staff. At first, Radcliffe was camera-shy. He wasn't convinced that he had the chops to pull it off. Like many people who are feeling insecure or shy, he laughed it off with some self-deprecating humour in an attempt to remove himself from the hot seat. I didn't let him, and we pushed on. After the videos were released to the company, he was showered with praise. One of the videos ended up being circulated nationally. Radcliffe began to see what I had understood since we met: that there was so much more just beneath his gruff veteran surface.

Radcliffe was a former air weapons technician. He'd risen through the ranks of the Royal Canadian Armed Forces and had done the same in the security company he was now leading. On top of that, he was a father of two who established and ran a hockey camp for families experiencing financial and cultural barriers. He was a busy man. By most standards he was already successful, providing for his family and making a difference in the city he lived in. However, as Radcliffe put it, "[*The Art of Doing*] has transformed my life and helped me find a different definition of success."

Although Radcliffe was a senior executive with a large multinational firm, highly regarded within his field, he was miserable. Post-traumatic stress disorder (PTSD), a condition triggered by scary, shocking, or dangerous events, was responsible for some of that. The other part, I suspect, was from burying his passions over the years.

Radcliffe and I started to dig into why he wasn't burning as brightly as he could be. We started hanging out outside of work, and I began to see a different side of him. At first he was guarded and reluctant to share much with me, which meant his journey of self-discovery remained stalled. But the rocket ignited when he sang his first karaoke song at my house! *The soldier can sing!* I thought to myself, and he seemed to enjoy it, too. We continued singing together occasionally and also started exploring other activities he believed "were for other people, not soldiers." From playing instruments to exploring photography, from sketching to writing, he tried as many things as he could. Leading with curiosity and having no set destination, we continued to ask *what if?* We discovered Radcliffe had many creative skills that had been lying dormant—ungerminated seeds waiting for some light and warmth, and thirsting for attention.

Over the span of two years, Damian has gone from being a private karaoke singer with no idea how to play the guitar to a performer, recording artist and writer. "[Without *The Art of Doing* tools] I would have gone my entire life miserably ignorant to the hidden passion and talent I had for music," Damian told me.

One of my favourite things about this story is that Radcliffe was a "grown-up." We often assume that middle-aged folks have already discovered everything about themselves, that they no longer need to ask *what if?* We believe that new ventures, especially creative ones, are for younger people. However, Radcliffe, with a full and busy life, leaned into the exercise of asking *what if?* and found a new source of happiness and purpose. His children now see another side of their father, perhaps a more vulnerable one. They get to watch him struggle, fail and persist in the pursuit of passion, which is so important. Better yet, they have gotten to be part of his metamorphosis.

Watching Radcliffe leap outside of his comfort zone and discover new talents has been a profound experience for everyone who has had the joy of witnessing it.

A JOURNEY WITHIN

Genevive Powell is the founder of Shakti Holistic Health, a coaching business that helps people live a happy and healthy life in alignment with their highest self. When Powell pitched her business idea to me in 2022, I loved it and wanted to help her actualize it in any way I could. We'd been discussing her new company in passing for several years. Every time we chatted I would ask about her plan and next steps. As often happens with big dreams, time had passed but the project hadn't budged. Since we were familiar with each other, I didn't pull too many punches. I'd consistently ask about her social media presence and the time she was taking to brand her business idea. I'd question how much time she was putting into her jobs as a server versus the time and effort she was putting into her new career. She'd always respond that the serving job gave her the money she needed to pay the bills and eat.

When she told me that she needed the serving gigs, she

was also telling me that she didn't believe she could earn that money (or more) from her business idea. That lack of belief kept her from progressing to where she could canvas for clients and ask them to pay for her services. Without paying clients, she obviously wouldn't be able to support herself with the new venture.

In 2023, Powell signed on as one of my clients. We embarked on discovering the real reasons why she was reluctant to take her foot off first base and sprint to second. The irony that she wanted to guide other people in health and wellness while feeling stuck in her own life wasn't lost on either of us. Powell had done 95 percent of the work already: she had paid for her certifications, mapped out her business, created branding material and walked her holistic living talk. She was only missing that final and imperative ingredient: belief in herself. Once we were able to uncover the issues that were holding her back, we could then deal with and move through them so she could confidently move forward with her dream business.

Says Powell: "Working with *The Art of Doing* allowed me to confront some of the shadows and fears that were blocking me from taking the next steps with my business. It helped me to see through the false narratives and gave me the confidence and reassurance that I was on the right path in the moments that I doubted myself. It taught me how to break down bigger goals into more realistic steps and take action so I didn't feel overwhelmed by the thought of taking on too much. It challenged me to grow in ways I didn't think I could, and pushed me in the direction of success. My business wouldn't be in the place it is today without your guidance and I am very grateful for your support along my journey."

I cannot overstate the joy I feel when I see a client experience that lightbulb moment after applying just a few of the tools from *The Art of Doing* to their lives. Not only does it make me feel good, but it also reinforces how important it is for me to continue to use the tools as I move forward with my own projects.

DOCUMENTING THE
FOLLOW-THROUGH

I first met Alex Eskandarkhah, an Iranian-Canadian filmmaker and entrepreneur, in my office in 2020. At that time he was just beginning his journey in film. I was invigorated by his appetite for knowledge and desire to learn. He reminded me a lot of myself at his age—hungry, ambitious and quick-moving. He told me about an idea he had for a documentary about a blackballed basketball coach, Don "Tex" Phillips, who had moved from the U.S. to Alberta to take the reins of a Canadian college team. His squad became the subject of sabotage on their way to back-to-back titles, before Phillips's premature exit as head coach. I'd heard about Phillips, and I thought that Eskandarkhah's idea had legs. I was excited to see what the project could turn into.

I started by asking Eskandarkhah some very basic questions to get a sense of how prepared he was, how much he knew and how far along the process he was. When pitching projects, it's imperative you have a well-thought-out treatment to show potential partners, which is kind of like a lookbook that takes the reader through all the essential elements of the project (plot, team, funding, etc.). I asked to see his, and he told me that he didn't have one. I later found out how deeply our talk had affected him: "Why not? Why hadn't I written a treatment yet? He was asking me the most basic of questions that had everything to do with doing as opposed to the glamorization of the idea. That question prompted me to go home that night and write a twenty-page treatment for my documentary, which ended up becoming *Coaching While Black*."

Eskandarkhah credits our conversation as the catalyst he needed to create more: "[That] conversation . . . put a battery in my back when it came to execution. Doing. I saw someone who was doing at a high level with zero compromises. [Jesse] stood for what he believed in, he loved what he was doing, and he was doing everything he could to lead by example. Jesse's philosophy has become mine in a lot of ways. Since then, his impact on me has had a domino effect on the impact and success I've been able to have—something I could never have imagined sitting in Jesse's office that day. *The Art of Doing* is an inspiration for anyone looking to excel in their personal and professional lives with love and grace."

I love watching the rest of the world experience something

that may never have seen the light of day had it not been for the hard work of someone practising *The Art of Doing*. I feel like a proud parent.

LIVE IN THE DREAM

I was a mentor to Sean Lesko when he was in his first year of university. We were introduced by a friend of his who had attended a presentation of mine and, later, an acting workshop. The two friends had started a production company together and were eager to learn from someone with experience in the business. As I worked with this team of young men, I noticed that Lesko seemed a bit more keen to go deeper. We would frequently discuss his projects and dreams, and after hearing what I had to say, he'd often push back on the techniques that seemed too simple to be effective. Later he'd come around, realizing that those tools might have some weight.

Full disclosure: Lesko ended up renting a room in my Edmonton townhouse for a while. While convenient for him, it also meant we were able to spend a substantial amount of time discussing *The Art of Doing*. Lesko could see that he was overcomplicating his process, often looking for the more difficult and treacherous routes to his dream, and really appreciated the new approach we were taking: "*The Art of Doing* does a great job of organizing and explaining the simple, but not easy, wisdom compiled from what feels like a couple of lifetimes of experience."

Lesko is an actor, producer and writer currently doing his best to make a name for himself in the business. He developed imposter syndrome, camera shyness and work anxiety after the pandemic and subsequent union strike slowed the entertainment industry. Even though he knew the steps and the tools he needed to employ to counter those feelings, he still found himself making excuses and looking for the exit door. As he put it: "I knew I needed reps, so I signed up for a class to get me back in front of the camera again. I was so afraid of working with a talented Vancouver-based pool of actors and taking criticism from a longtime working acting coach. What if they found out? What if I was not an actor who deserved to be there? All of this anxiety crept up on me. Before my first class, I ordered an Uber, which would have gotten me to class fifteen minutes early, as the email specified we should be. My first Uber was cancelled on me, so I ordered another. My Uber app was crashing and glitching out my phone, so I missed the next one, and I ended up having to uninstall the app, reinstall the app, and reboot my phone. I was already late for class. The fear and negative mind chatter came after me. 'You're already late. It's okay. You can go next week.' All these thoughts aimed at preventing me from facing my fears and social anxiety. I almost didn't go. I was fifteen minutes late to class, but, as it turned out, so was everybody else. My knees were shaking during our first take, but the second take was better. I didn't like the work that I had done that night, but I was proud of myself for doing it. After eight weeks of work, I had built up enough confidence to rid myself of camera shyness, dust the rust off of my acting skills, and have truly levelled up. I owe all of it to my belief in myself, even when my inner monologue was pitted against me . . . *The Art of Doing* is an amazing blueprint to teach you tools that will inevitably force you to grow out of your comfort zone, and realize your greatest aspirations, should you decide to be courageous enough to implement them."

Lesko has always been an inquisitive and argumentative student of *The Art of Doing*. He would push back and question a lot. However, once he gained a personal understanding of a concept or tool, he would always integrate it into his life. His personal growth through the process has been amazing to watch, and I continue to admire his courage as he advances on his goals and dreams.

STRATEGIC LEAPS

I got to know Janine Stowe when she worked on the first #MakeItAwkward Summit with me. Stepping into our small and scrappy team collaborating around my kitchen table to pull together our inaugural conference, it quickly became clear that she is a "doer." Resourceful and dedicated, she's not afraid to roll up her sleeves and take on new and challenging projects. However, despite her gusto, she often struggled to push forward with her own ventures.

Stowe and I have had countless conversations about the many areas she could apply her skills and gain a competitive advantage. Yet *The Art of Doing* initially made her uncomfortable. "As an established designer and systems thinker, I naturally examine situations from a 360-degree perspective. But as a self-proclaimed perfectionist, I often find myself mired in the details—endlessly weighing options and stalling to the point of paralysis. While thorough research and a strategic plan are

indispensable, the act of 'doing' is crucial for enacting change."
But as we know, for many like Stowe, that's easier said than done.

Stowe is both creative and highly practical. She has an innate ability to anticipate the needs of her clients and an uncanny knack for asking the right questions to get to the heart of a problem. She cuts to the chase with detail, care and efficiency. Her thoughtful and detail-oriented approach serves her and her clients well, but it was also one of the things she felt was preventing her from propelling forward. After completing her Master of Design program in strategic foresight and innovation from OCAD University, she was eager to launch a new business. Inspired by the principles of *The Art of Doing*, she decided to take a chance and not wait for someone else's permission. She took the leap and started School-Hub.

Stowe recalls: "I recently stepped out of my comfort zone and launched a business I had long contemplated but kept on the back burner. In a single day, I drafted a business plan, registered my company, and set up a website, boldly announcing my new venture on LinkedIn to ensure I stayed committed. For me, *The Art of Doing* doesn't mean you have to jump in headfirst; it just means you need to jump."

ACKNOWLEDGEMENTS

I am overwhelmed with gratitude for the many individuals who have played an instrumental role in bringing this book to life. The realization of this work would not have been possible without the unwavering support, encouragement and guidance from the incredible people who have touched my life in various ways.

To my beloved family, whose love and encouragement have been the cornerstone of my endeavours, I am eternally grateful. Your belief in me even when I doubted myself has been a constant source of strength. Your sacrifices and patience are a testament to the power of family bonds. To my mother, Monica Lipscombe, thank you for showing me that through adversity and pain there can always be light. Thank you for continuing the strong traditions of keeping the family close and always opening up your home for us all to come back to, regardless of where we are in the world. To my dad, Richard Lipscombe, thank you for your consistent and unwavering love. Your dedication to what you believe in and your passion for creation is one of the best gifts you ever could have passed on to me. To my big brother, Curtis Lipscombe, thank you for being my friend and sharing your passion for music with me from an early age. I still remember telling you "Turn it down!" because you always had the hottest hits playing after school. Some of that early music love was definitely passed on. Keep on making music—the world deserves to hear it. To Deanne McIntyre, my sister and best friend, you have always been my number-one fan, and I am so proud of you. I love watching you create a life and business around what you truly believe in; you are changing people's lives every day. To my wife, Julia LeConte Lipscombe, there aren't enough words to express my gratitude for everything you do to support me and the family as my life takes twists and turns. Our life is wonderful, and I am so excited to see what new chapters we get to crush together. I can't stress how beneficial it's been to have such a skilled writer and critic in my corner. Julia, you have shaped and continue to shape the man I am today, and I owe so much of my literary success to your guidance. To my children—Chile, Tripp and Indiana Lipscombe—you three beautiful boys make my life worth living. You may not ever know it until you have kids of your own, but you have saved my life over and over again. I am so in love with all three of you and so proud to be your dad.

My gratitude extends to the dedicated team at HarperCollins, who saw the potential in this project and tirelessly worked alongside me to refine and shape it. Your expertise, keen insights and commitment to the craft have elevated this book beyond my wildest dreams. It doesn't seem that long ago that Brad Wilson and I were having coffee at Soho trying to figure out what this book would be. Thank you for sticking with me and helping me get this book out into the world.

To my speaking agent, Jeff Lohnes, if there were a global agent award ceremony, you'd get my vote. I love all my agents, but you have a way of collaborating with me and eliminating problems when they arrive with such grace. I'm lucky to have you and can't wait to see what we do next. To my entertainment agent, Sarah Davis, thank you for representing me and introducing me to the Vancouver scene of film and TV. I am so happy our paths crossed and can't wait to get back on set and make some more magic together. To my former sports agent, Kris Mychasiw, thanks for taking me on so many years ago and opening my world to the world of professional athletics. I'll never forget the cockpit ride from the islands. To my first acting agent, Elisabeth Ebbels, thank you for your love and tutelage that still continues to this day.

To my teachers and mentors, whose wisdom and guidance have paved the way for my growth as a writer and a person, I owe a debt of gratitude. Your lessons, critiques and words of encouragement have been invaluable stepping stones on this creative journey. Your belief in my potential has been a driving force in overcoming obstacles and embracing challenges. To my teacher and coach, John Dedrick, you have shaped so much for me over the years—initially as my coach, who I looked up to and craved attention from; to my teacher, who spoke my language; and now as a colleague I can call on and shoot the shit with. You have impacted so many of the student-athletes that have crossed your path, but I feel extra lucky that I can still call you a friend. To my former track coach, Linda Blade, we went through *a lot* together, and I can honestly say I am grateful for it all. My favourite memories were our outdoor training sessions, when we would talk for hours about any and every problem in the world and try to solve them. You challenged me to think differently and question everything—thank you.

I am indebted to the numerous inspirations who have coloured the tapestry of my imagination. From the authors whose words ignited my passion for storytelling, to the artists whose visuals stirred my creativity, to my family and friends who lit a fire in my soul, you have all influenced this book. Your authenticity has kindled the flame within me, propelling me to explore uncharted territories of thought and expression. A special shout-out to my late Uncle Brett, who fearlessly led with his heart and his art. You helped me believe that I could create without anyone's permission, and I am eternally grateful for it. To my dear friend Isaac Ikram, we have been friends for decades and I have looked up to you since day one. That hasn't stopped, and I doubt it ever will. You are a testament to all the good there is in the world, and I hope to be a little more like you every day. To Janine and Johnny, your friendship has been so monumental in the creation of the life I have always wanted. It doesn't matter where in the world you live, my family's lives are more complete because you two are in them! I can't wait for our next adventure. To my friend and singing coach, Ellory Clayton, thank you for always believing in me and my voice, especially when I did not believe in it myself. You continue to give me confidence to play, experiment and enjoy the gift of song. Dino Bottos, thank you for your support and help through a really messy time. To my Morehouse brothers—Donvongee, Terrence, Jansen, Dave, Keith, Steve, Corey, Pope, Ramsey, Glen and Savoy—thank you.

Lastly, to the readers who will embark on this journey with me, thank you. Your curiosity and engagement give life to these pages. It is my deepest hope that the words contained herein resonate with you, inspire you and perhaps even leave a lasting impact on your own creative endeavours.

In the end, this book stands as a collective effort, a testament to the power of collaboration, love, belief and human connection. To all those mentioned and the countless others who have played a part, thank you from the bottom of my heart. May the echoes of your contributions reverberate within these pages and beyond.

With heartfelt gratitude,
Jesse Lipscombe